MY BAGS ARE IN THE BACK

Captain Peter Galloway
Royal Navy

Copyright © Peter Galloway 2017
This book is sold subject to the condition that it shall not, by way of trade or otherwise, be lent, resold, hired out, or otherwise circulated without the publisher's prior consent in any form of binding or cover other than that in which it is published and without a similar condition including this condition being imposed on the subsequent publisher.
The moral right of Peter Galloway has been asserted.
ISBN-13: 978-1544004495
ISBN-10: 1544004494

This is a work of creative nonfiction. While all the stories in this book are true, some names and identifying details have been changed to protect the privacy of the people involved.

CONTENTS

AUTHOR'S PREFACE v

1943 TO 1961 - WHY THE NAVY? 1
   Introduction 1
   The Admiralty Interview Board 5

1961/62 - BRNC DARTMOUTH 6
   My first unfortunate words 6
   The Dartmouth Training Squadron 8
      The Cape Verde Islands 11
      Crossing The Atlantic 13
      The Snifter Suction Cock Valve Disaster 14
      Barbados 17
      British Guiana 18

1962/63 - MIDSHIPMAN'S YEAR 21
   The flight to Singapore 21
   Six months in HMS ARK ROYAL 23
      Perth, Australia 25
      Setting fire to a Royal Marine Major 26
      The rugger match against the All Blacks 27
      Revising for the Fleet Board 28
      A flight deck disaster 29
      A day in the main galley 33
      P 1127 – The world's first deck landing 34
   A week in HMS MARYTON, 17 - 22 Sep 1962 36
      A very unusual sign on the funnel 37
      Sunset Ceremony – A total shambles 38
      The minesweeping exercise – Where's the Officer-of-the-Watch? 39
      Defaulters – The seaman, the cook and the fine. 40

A week in HMS OTTER, 6 – 12 Jan 1963 43

Six months in HMS ESKIMO 45

   Ship Handling *45*

   Safe-cracking *47*

   Three men in a boat *48*

   Sailing close to the wind *50*

1963-1967 - ROYAL NAVAL ENGINEERING COLLEGE (RNEC) ... 51

   Dirty deeds in my 1938 MG TA *52*

   The run ashore and the police sergeant *54*

1969-1971 - HMS HAMPSHIRE 57

   A one week joining routine *57*

   A 'phone call home from Cape Horn *63*

1971/72 - SOUTHAMPTON UNIVERSITY - MSC 64

   The sparking plug, the bus stop and the pensioner *64*

   The card reader and the printout *66*

1972 – 1974 - ADMIRALTY SURFACE WEAPONS ESTABLISHMENT (ASWE) 68

   A Lieutenant docks a destroyer *70*

   The immigration problem at Heathrow *72*

   An offer to become a Polaris Systems Officer *73*

1975-1977 - HMS ACHILLES 76

   The Hong Kong dinner jacket *76*

   An emergency surgical operation off Vietnam. *78*

   The Brazilian lacy tops *80*

   Collision at sea *82*

   Supermarket trollies in Cowes *86*

   A brief visit to Rockall *88*

   Diving in Tromso harbour *92*

   How not to talk to your Captain *95*

1978/79 - HMS CENTURION 98

   The Functional Costing System – Three years into two *98*

1979 - ADMIRALTY UNDERWATER WEAPONS ESTABLISHMENT (AUWE) 100

Memories of the spy story of 1961 – the year I joined the Navy 100

1980/1981 - MOD, DIRECTORATE NAVAL MANAGEMENT SYSTEMS, DATA PROCESSING POLICY 104

The Garden Party at Buckingham Palace 106
A breakdown in Parliament Square 107

1982-1983 - HMS GLAMORGAN 109

Exocet concerns 111
The first day at war 114
The Pebble Island raid 116
The radar that choked itself to death 119
The unfortunate Action Stations alarm 121
The Chinese Laundryman who tried to jump ship 123
The Rapier missile system on the hill 126
The Mexican Commander in the wardroom 129
Return to UK 132
Support from the counties of Glamorgan – The cheque 137
Support from the counties of Glamorgan – The cheers 139
Support from the counties of Glamorgan – The cheeky 141
The Welsh Guards Major comes visiting 142
Put the Commander's bed out will you 143
A flight into Beirut 145

1984/86 - MOD, NAVAL SECRETARY, WEAPON ENGINEERING APPOINTER 149

The day that the American Secretary of State came to lunch 151
The senior submarine Commander and his final appointment 153
An interview without coffee for a colleague 155
Lunch at Simpson's-in-the-Strand and the unexpected consequence ... 157

1986/87 - THE ADMIRALTY INTERVIEW BOARD (AIB) 159

A histrionic effect echoed around the hangar 160
A candidate has a nasty fall 161

1988 - NATIONAL DEFENCE COLLEGE, NEW DELHI 162

Day One in India - Clearing Customs *164*
How to make ice cubes in India *167*
The day the front door caught fire *169*
The exploding radiogram *170*
Some Indian road signs and a crocodile warning *172*
We nearly lost an Air Commodore *174*

1989 - MOD, ORDNANCE BOARD 177

1990 / 1992 - MOD, DIRECTORATE OF SCIENCE (SEA) 179

The unforgettable US Marine Colonel *179*
Desert Storm *181*
The American breakfast *182*

1993-95 - NAVAL ADVISER TO BRITISH HIGH COMMISSIONER, NEW DELHI 184

A dinner for eight Victoria Cross holders *184*
White-water rafting on the Ganges *190*
The SAS come to stay for a month *193*
Lynn's driving skills in Delhi *196*
The striped croquet lawn *201*
The cocktail party with a distinctive aroma *202*
The Delhi Driving Test *204*
The Defence Services Staff College - Quetta to Wellington *206*
A Visit to Ootacamund (Ooty) and the rules of Snooker *214*
Bilateral exercise with Indian Navy and the Lakkshadweeps *217*
Postscript and the end of my Naval career *223*

AUTHOR'S CAREER SUMMARY 224

AUTHOR'S PREFACE

I started writing this short book in November 2015, approaching my 72nd birthday, when I realised that my children and grandchildren had not got the faintest idea what I had been up to during the 35 years I had spent in the Royal Navy. Later, as the draft took shape, I recognised that there was additional and fascinating material of possible interest to a greater audience, both young and old.

The book explains, briefly, what led me towards a career in the senior service and then describes, in chronological order, the more humorous or significant events in the various appointments ashore and afloat.

It is intended that the reader should enjoy the, hopefully, amusing anecdotes, find other parts educational from a historical perspective and others which give an insight into life on board a warship in the second half of the twentieth century.

A Health Warning. There are a few, very few, naughty words in some anecdotes and I beg the reader's forbearance and understanding that life in a warship does expose one to the language of the day, shall we call it. There aren't too many!

During my naval career I did not keep a diary or record of events and the writing of the book has been a matter of recollection, often assisted by looking through old photograph albums. Accordingly, some events may have suffered from the inevitable clouding effect through the mist of time, but I hope I will be forgiven if the odd mistake is spotted by anyone who shared any of the experiences.

I realised, whilst writing about particular events, that references to individuals by name was not always appropriate, perhaps because they had found the incident less amusing than my recollection or some such reason and to that end, I have omitted a lot of names by design.

I was also very conscious and concerned, when writing about my time in HMS GLAMORGAN during the Falklands conflict, about showing respect for the members of the ship's company who did not return home after the Exocet attack on 12th June 1982, and for their loved ones. The only time I felt overcome by emotion during the 3½ months we were involved, was when we returned to Portsmouth to be greeted by thousands of family members on the jetty, including some whose sons or husbands or brothers had not returned and who were seeking final reassurance that we 'had not made a mistake' about the names.

I must mention my wife, Lynn's contribution to the book and my career. When I retired from the Navy, the First Sea Lord, as was the custom, wrote a long letter summarising the Naval Staff's perception of my career. In this letter, Sir Jock Slater, in the traditional green ink of an Admiral, summarised my final appointment by writing some very splendid comments, but the ones that need to be recorded here, concern Lynn:

Overall, you made a significant contribution to the improvement in Defence Relations between the United Kingdom and India. You and Lynn excelled on the diplomatic circuit, carrying out your duties with flair and style; the Board is especially grateful to Lynn for her sterling support during this testing appointment and indeed throughout your career.

1943 TO 1961 - WHY THE NAVY?

Introduction

In the second World War my father had been manning a radar assisted Ack-Ack unit at Rame Head, overlooking Plymouth Sound, when he met and later married a lovely girl from the nearby village of Cawsand. Years later, on 16th December 1943, I caused that 'lovely lady' some distress as I checked in at 11lb, a fact which she has reminded me of, periodically. The birth was a great family affair in my maternal Grandparents' Cawsand home, "The Woodlands", a fabulous four-storied house overlooking the village.

My Grandparents house, The Woodlands, Cawsand.

Apart from my own involvement in this event, the other immediate members of the family involved included my Grandmother, since I was born in her bed, my mother for obvious reasons, and my Aunty Peggy as midwife. Gran's bedroom faced South East and looked directly across the Sound to the Great Mew Stone.

It seems unlikely that this view across the sea to the Mew Stone was imprinted on my memory, as I emerged, but for some obscure reason that view is still an important part of my life today.

The Mewstone viewed from The Woodlands.

The family was very involved in the war at that time with all four uncles in the Armed Forces, including my godfather, uncle Peter, after whom I was named, because my parents were concerned for his safety as a young Lancaster pilot. Peter was awarded the DFM at the age of twenty, and clocked up 700 flying hours before his 21st birthday. Between August 1942 and February 1943, he completed a full tour of 30 operations with 207 Squadron, which lost 154 crews during WW II. Later, he served throughout the war and for a total of 37 years RAF service.

My Grandfather had retired from the Royal Navy many years before I was born but was recalled for the war while uncle John (Ted) was still serving in the RN, as was uncle Michael, while uncle Ken was in the Army.

With fifteen cousins on that side of the family, holidays and Christmases at Cawsand were memorable and fantastic fun. The hall was decorated with a twenty-five foot Christmas tree and the house lent itself to the production of a Christmas show, which the poor parents had, of course, to endure. This involved the actors, aged between about five and ten, assembling in the dark and cold, on the long veranda at the front of the house, climbing through the sitting-room bay windows and waiting behind the twelve-foot tall curtains for the show to commence. The excitement was palpable although the productions were an endurance test for the long-suffering parents.

Summer holidays were equally memorable with days on the pebble beaches of Cawsand and Kingsand and rowing boat trips out to Rame Head, interspersed with trips to the expansive sandy beaches in Whitsand Bay, particularly down the cliff to Freathy beach. On one particular day, when unusually the sun was not very evident and a sea mist had descended, we young cousins were grumbling and saying we wanted to go back to Gran's house. Uncle Ken rounded on us.

"I brought you down here to enjoy yourselves and enjoy yourselves you jolly well will!"

Ken, like all of the uncles, was keen to get us out in a boat and on one occasion, he took four of us very young cousins out in a small rowing boat to the lighthouse on Plymouth breakwater, ostensibly to take the three lighthouse-keepers some fresh vegetables. The two mile return trip to Cawsand proved problematical when the wind rose and we had to row extremely hard to make any way. While uncle Ken manned two oars, we children took turns on the other two oars and received a severe blast whenever we caught a crab. We laughed but Ken found it less amusing.

It was no surprise that five of the cousins joined the Armed Forces later in life, three rising to RN Captain, one to Lieutenant Colonel in the Royal Marines and one to Lieutenant Colonel in the Army. My Grandfather had retired from the Royal Navy many years before I was born but he had a great influence over my life and he amongst other things encouraged me to take up woodcarving at the age of sixteen. However, the incident that possibly swayed me in my decision to join the Navy may well have happened earlier, when I was nearly five.

HMS Vanguard, the 45,000-ton battleship was launched when I was one year old, but from July 1947 until August 1948 she was in refit in Devonport Dockyard preparing to take the Royal Family on a tour of Australia and New Zealand in January 1949. Unfortunately, the King was later too ill to travel and the tour was indefinitely postponed. However, whilst the battleship was in dry dock, Grandpa managed to arrange a tour of the ship for the two of us and the memory of walking under the keel of this 818ft long leviathan with a 108ft beam is still imprinted on my memory. Equally impressive was the walk up the forecastle beneath four massive barrels of her two 15-inch turrets. I say "up" the fo'c'sle advisedly, because it was indeed a climb up the deck, rising about twenty feet, as I remember it, from A-turret up to the prow. Perhaps something was being formed in my mind at this very young age.

Ten years later, the next influence towards a Naval career was cousin Jonathan, three years older than me, who was serving as a Sub-Lieutenant in a cruiser, HMS BERMUDA, in Portsmouth in the late '50s. He showed me around the ship and we ended up in the wardroom for a chat. Being lunchtime, I remember a very smart naval steward approaching us as we sat there in enormous leather armchairs with the fans rotating above us.

"A drink Sir?" he asked.

Jonathan replied, "Thank you, a gin and tonic please."

The steward turned to the young civilian 15 year-old and raised an eyebrow. "And you Sir?"

"The same for me please," I replied.

This is the life I thought - I might have to give this a try. Hmm! Not perhaps the best reason for pursuing a vocational career, but...

I recall that a few weeks later Jonathan's cruiser visited Plymouth and I was at the Woodlands in Cawsand with the rest of my family. He called in to see the grandparents and stated that he would wave as the cruiser left Plymouth the following morning at 0730 and was due to round the breakwater at about 0800. When I pointed out that the ship would be some two miles from the house and the chance of seeing him "wave" were pretty slim, he replied, "Just keep an eye out and keep your fingers crossed."

The next morning as she rounded the breakwater and headed past Cawsand, I waited and was not disappointed, as a white sheet appeared, stretched between two scuttles, somewhere aft and waved up and down in the wind. There is no doubt that I had been enormously impressed by the esprit de corps, efficiency, smartness and general professionalism of those I had met on board the cruiser and here was an example, perhaps, of the way the Navy enjoyed life.

The Admiralty Interview Board

Some time later, having decided to apply for entry to the Britannia Royal Naval College at Dartmouth, I travelled down to Gosport from the family home in the Cotswolds, to the Admiralty Interview Board. The interview lasted three days, involving written tests, practical tasks, leadership challenges and a final face-to-face interview with a board comprising a Naval Captain, a Headmaster, a Wren Officer and a Naval Commander. All went reasonably well until the last few moments when the Captain, the President of the Board[1] looked down at his paperwork and said, "You're very young, in fact right on the limits for Cadet Entry into Dartmouth. What will you do if I say you have to reapply in one year's time?"

"Join the Army," I replied.

They let me in.

---

[1] Little did I realize that some twenty-seven years later I was to be the President of a Board interviewing prospective officers.

1961/62 - BRNC DARTMOUTH

My first unfortunate words

In September 1961, and not yet eighteen, I arrived at Kingswear railway station on the eastern side of the river Dart and looked up at the imposing façade of BRNC Dartmouth. My train had arrived some half an hour after the arrival of the train from London, bringing the majority of my fellow Cadets to the College. I took the ferry across the river to Dartmouth and looked for a taxi to take me up to the College with my luggage. We drove up the hill, arriving at the mast in front of the vast parade ground.

The driver asked me where I wanted to be dropped off and seeing about a hundred young men formed up in groups with their luggage, nearer to the main building, I replied, "Over there with them, I suppose."

"I'm not driving on the parade ground – no way," replied the driver.

So I said: "Well pull over here then." He did and I suspect one wheel may well have crossed the invisible line marking the limit of the parade ground.

As I looked up, I saw an extremely smartly dressed naval chap approaching the taxi with some sort of stick under his armpit and a peaked cap, which seemed to be rather low on his forehead. As I opened the door of the taxi, which was rather ancient, having doors, which opened 'backwards', it caught the naval chap unawares, amid-drift. As he regained his breath and composure, I uttered my first words in the Royal Navy, "My bags are in the back."

Needless to say, I had not recognized the Chief GI of the College, who ruled his domain, the parade ground, with a rod of steel and sense of propriety, which was unparalleled on this planet. He was speechless, but only for a split second. From that moment and for the next four weeks, my feet didn't touch the ground. Every moment of my waking day, he was there, shouting, "Double." I ran from 0600, when we awoke until pipe down every night. He would find me coming out of a classroom, the gymnasium, the swimming pool or sailing, down on the river, and run me to my next assignment.

For the first four weeks we were not permitted to stray from the College grounds and it was with some considerable relief that we first sampled the pubs of Dartmouth in mid-October. As I entered the Market Place pub, that first evening, I could scarcely believe it as I saw the Chief in the other bar, beckoning me to approach. "Yes Chief," I said.

"Young Sir, I want to buy you a pint. The other GIs and I have had so much fun thinking about your entrance to naval life, that you deserve a drink."

The Dartmouth Training Squadron

The first term passed quickly and then we went to sea in the Dartmouth Training Squadron (DTS). There were four ships in the squadron and I joined the Type 15 frigate, HMS WIZARD, together with nineteen other Cadets and twenty Midshipmen. We all shared a mess-deck, right aft beneath the quarterdeck, with the Midshipmen on the port side and the Cadets to starboard. A few slept in bunks but the majority of us were in hammocks, slung one above the other across the mess.

The idea behind the DTS was that young officers should experience life on the lower deck; work in each and every department as a Rating and certainly not experience any of the niceties of life in the wardroom. Twenty Midshipmen and twenty Cadets, including myself, joined HMS WIZARD in Plymouth.

HMS WIZARD - Type 15 Frigate
Commissioned March 1944 as a W-Class destroyer. Converted to Type 15 Frigate in 1954. In 1957 refitted to join the Dartmouth Training Squadron. Sold for scrap in February 1967. Length: 358ft. Beam: 38ft. Draught: 14ft. Complement: 180. Displacement: 2,300 tons.

MY BAGS ARE IN THE BACK

HMS WIZARD was built in the year I was born and after service around the world, including in the Suez crisis, she was converted from a W-Class destroyer into a frigate in 1953/4. At around 2000 tons, it occurred to me that she was 1/25th the size of the VANGUARD and our ship's company of 180, including the forty of us, was 1/10th the size of the battleship's.

We sailed from Plymouth early in 1962, bound for Gibraltar and the West Indies, but first we had to run the gauntlet of the Bay of Biscay in January. The Cadets and Midshipmen in the mess-deck right aft, had to fetch all of their meals from the galley amidships and to this end, each half of our mess provided a messman every day to fetch the food in a mess "fanny", an aluminium rectangular pot with a handle, of sufficient size to hold twenty portions of the meal. The galley is always sited amidships in an attempt to minimize the heave effect of a ship's motion, whereas the messes right for'd or aft suffer the full effect of massive vertical movement as the ship struggles over the rollers of a storm at sea.

It was quite a trip even to get from the mess, up a ladder to the anti-submarine mortars sited for'd of the quarterdeck, then up again to the main passageway through the ship, termed, in Plymouth-based ships, the Armada Way, to the galley. One day, when I was messman for the Cadets' mess, I set off with the fanny, bouncing off bulkheads and staggering up the ladder to join the queue of sailors from the other messes, the gunners, the stokers, the seamen and so on.

Apart from learning the ins and outs of this way of feeding the ship's company, termed broadside messing, we also picked up a new form of the English language. This was where I learnt how sailors manage to inject the f... word inside other words to great effect. Sailors were adept in the art and it took a while to decode some of the extremely long words they concocted. The word 'fantastic' for instance would almost double in length, when the additional swear word was inserted.

There was always a humorous side to life in the queue at the galley and Jolly Jack can be relied upon to coin jokes and phrases that summarise a situation pithily and appropriately. I recall, after a couple of weeks on board, waiting my turn, when from the front of the queue came, "Cor blimey chef – if I have any more of your b... chips, I'll have a square…"

Back to the point of this memory of life on board this frigate. I was lucky enough never to suffer from seasickness in my 35 years in the Navy, but this was definitely not the case for some of the Cadets and Midshipmen as we crossed the Bay of Biscay that day, our first day at sea. It was probably no more than a force eight gale but fifteen of the Cadets definitely did not want any lunch, one particular day.

I was duty messman and fought my way through the wind and spray past the mortars to the galley, to get the stew, the easiest meal to prepare in rough weather. As I returned and looked down into the mortar well on the port side, I saw two Cadets leaning over the side, one for'd of the mortar and the other twenty feet further aft. They were definitely not studying the wave formation.

It was a matter of tradition that we all wore officers caps on the upper deck and they were both correctly dressed for the occasion. As the Cadet furthest for'd leant further outboard in an attempt not to decorate his uniform with what we termed a Technicolor yawn, his cap was wrenched from him by the gale. As it hit the sea, it floated with the inside of the cap facing the heavens. In the split second that it took the cap to pass beneath the second Cadet, he too decided to yawn overboard. Unbelievably his production was a perfect hit, right into the cap. At this, the situation resembled a scene from a Whitehall farce, as the first Cadet turned to the second and yelled, "Do you mind?"

Returning to the mess-deck, the stew slopping around the fanny and thereby filling the mess with a delightfully strong smell of beef, onions and potatoes, my cheerful, "Lunch anyone?" was met with a chorus of moans and unrepeatable descriptions of my lineage.

The Cape Verde Islands

As we left the Bay in January 1962, we knew that the other half of the September 1961 BRNC entry, termed the Murray 2 entry, was due to join the DTS next term and they were due to visit the Baltic. We were therefore rather more than pleased to be heading for the warmth and excitement of the Caribbean. We headed south and visited the Cape Verde islands. These ten volcanic islands in the central Atlantic Ocean are some 350 miles off the coast of Western Africa and were uninhabited until the 15th century, when Portuguese explorers discovered and colonized the islands, establishing the first European settlement in the tropics.

Since independence in 1975, the islands are known as Cabo Verde, but in 1962 it was Cape Verde and there were extreme examples of poverty and starvation. HMS WIZARD was alongside and I was on duty in the middle watch one night as Bosun's Mate, a duty that included acting as tea/coffee/kai[2] maker for the Quartermaster.

I was alerted at 0200 by solid thump and subsequent moan about thirty feet from the gangway across the jetty. The Quartermaster asked me to investigate. As I crossed the jetty towards the fifteen-foot high concrete buttress protecting the jetty from the Atlantic seas, I saw in the gloom a young boy of about eight, lying spread-eagled and apparently lifeless on the jetty surface. It appeared that he had been asleep on the top of the wall and had fallen the fifteen feet onto concrete.

As I considered raising the medical team on-board, he opened his eyes and smiled! My Portuguese being rather limited, I asked him through sign language of a thumbs-up and a questioning eyebrow, whether he was 'ok'. He smiled again and indicated with fingers and thumb that he was hungry. At this, he got up and I took him across the jetty to the Quartermaster. We agreed that he should be fed and I was tasked to raid the galley. I returned with a newly baked loaf of bread about two feet long and five by five inches in section.

---

[2] Kai is traditional naval drink, particularly valued on a cold night in stormy weather, made with dark unsweetened chocolate, supplied in a large block and grated into a mug and boiling water applied.

Aware that he should not over-indulge on an empty stomach we tried to restrain him somewhat, but to no avail. He consumed the whole loaf and several cups of tea and when we went off watch at 0400, we handed him over to the next watch. He stayed with us for the next two days, doing odd jobs on the gangway, polishing brass and so on. I wish I could remember his real name, but I think we knew him as Paulo.

The point of this brief tale is that this was my first real awakening, as a very young Cadet, to the plight of people around the world. Later in life, as a senior officer, I was to serve in India and experience similar feelings for those less fortunate, but of course, by then I was older, wiser and had travelled the world. However, as an eighteen-year old, on my first travel experience outside the UK, Paulo served to educate me in a way that no academic training could provide. He was, despite all that he lacked, cheerful, funny, willing and resourceful. A lot of us decided that he may well have "fallen" on purpose, but if he had, he had displayed courage and initiative and we agreed that he deserved to be fed.

Crossing The Atlantic

In those days, a trip across the Atlantic in company with the three other frigates in the DTS, HMS ROEBUCK, VIGILANT and URCHIN involved a lot more than just steaming from A to B. Every day included exercises such as Man Overboard, Officer of the Watch Exercises for the trainees, Machinery Breakdowns and training lectures on every aspect of life at sea. We spent time with every department and I recall a very senior Chief Petty Officer delivering the Marine Engineering module. He spoke in a very considered and slow manner with a very deep voice.

"Galloway," he asked. "What do you think we use the 'Lub oil drain tank' for?"

"Could it be for storing the lub oil that we drain down?" I replied.

"Well done – quite right," he responded.

Realising that there might be further opportunities for a bit of fun, a fellow Cadet provided another similar moment when the Chief told us, "Tomorrow you will all be going down the Engine Room with the Engineer Officer and don't forget to wear your steaming boots and overalls and especially don't forget to wear your name tallies."

"Why do we have to wear our name tallies Chief?" asked the mischievous Cadet.

This baffled the Chief for a few moments, but he rallied. "That's a good question," he replied. "That is so the Engineer Officer can ask you your name (pause) and you can tell him and then (pause) he can look at your name tally to check you're right."

The Snifter Suction Cock Valve Disaster

During WWII, middle watch-keepers brewed up a concoction to stave off the cold and wet conditions experienced in Northern waters. The process involved scraping or grating a block of dark unsweetened chocolate into a pussers fanny[3], adding water and sugar, going easy on the water, such that the spoon would stand up on its own. The mixture would then be stuck under a steam drain in the boiler room until boiling hot and then taken to those on watch on the open bridge and the seamen acting as the watch-on-deck to man the sea boat if required, or to deal with any other requirement in the silent hours. This brew, known as Kai, or Kye, was still in use in the early sixties and very welcome, as I recall, when the spray and the occasional goffer, swept over the bridge on a very regular basis.

One night, as we crossed the Atlantic, the weather was fairly rough and the Petty Officer of the watch-on-deck, who were sheltering on the leeward side of the funnel near to the sea boat davits, decided that a brew-up was in order, and as usual, detailed off the youngest member of the watch to 'get a brew on'. It transpired that this was a first for the young seaman and the Petty Officer explained what needed to be done and where the air-lock entrance to the boiler-room was, for the final heating process. The lad set off to find a fanny and when he returned was given the block of chocolate, which he duly scraped with the pussers dirk that the Petty Officer kindly lent him. The cold water and sugar were added and he set off to find the boiler room four decks below.

The Leading Stoker on watch in the boiler room related what happened next after the deafening roar we all experienced a few minutes later. The seaman found the air-lock and clambered down into the heat and humidity of the inferno, known as the boiler room, a place he had never had the pleasure of visiting before. Recognising the senior watch-keeper to be the Chief Stoker, he timidly asked where he could stick the fanny to heat the Kai.

"Over there lad," growled the Chief, as he continued to tap the manometers and check the steam pressure. "You can't miss it. It's a

---

[3] Metal container, in this case a one gallon jug.

small pipe with a valve on it and you just stick it in the fanny for a minute. But don't open the valve too much or we'll all be sharing your brew."

In WIZARD's boiler room there were two Admiralty 3-drum water-tube boilers and the furnaces within them were lined with fire bricks, which transmitted the heat from the furnace fuel oil (FFO) burners to the water in the water tubes, to generate the steam which was then superheated to drive the turbines.

At the base of the boiler, which towered forty feet upwards into the gloomy upper reaches of the boiler space, was a small pipe with a simple valve to bleed off steam, before it was superheated, to heat the water for the endless cups of tea.

There was also a facility, on each boiler, to introduce oil into the furnace, to generate black smoke for the obvious reason of creating a smoke screen. This was achieved by placing a flexible pipe from a valve, known as the Snifter Suction Cock Valve, into a barrel of oil and opening the valve for a few seconds to create the required amount of smoke. I was told later that this valve had probably not been used since 1945.

The seaman approached the point indicated by the Chief Stoker as 'over there' and looked for the small pipe. He put the fanny down, inserted the pipe and tried to open the valve but this was not so simple since the valve appeared to be rusted and unused. He looked around to fine a shifter. Spotting a valve wrench of suitable weight, he gave the valve a tap and a wrench and cracked it open just a bit.

Three things then occurred almost simultaneously.

There was a loud shout from the Leading Stoker who was doing rounds of the boiler room recording the steam pressures. "Not that one you bl..."

The Kai mixture in the fanny disappeared in a split second.

The furnace, used to being fed a delicate combination of oil spray and air, received a gallon of cold water, causing the most dramatic effect as the immediate vaporisation of the water resulted in what can only be described as an enormously impressive rumbling explosion rather akin to a giant's tummy rumble followed by a sonorous belch.

Meanwhile, on the upper deck, the Petty Officer of the watch-on-deck and the rest of the watch got their ration of Kai in a rather unconventional manner as the vaporised Kai/FFO mixture descended from fifty feet above the funnel onto them and the best part of the superstructure abaft them.

The next morning, the Chief Stoker had to commission the second boiler so that the Kai-affected unit could cool down and the inside of the furnace and particularly the brickwork could be inspected for damage, which I am glad to say was not too severe. The First Lieutenant was not amused either when the full extent of the FFO spray covering every single part of the upper deck abaft the funnel was found to be particularly difficult to shift.

Barbados

On our first night in Barbados, we heard our first steel band, but not under conditions which the Cadets could particularly enjoy. The wardroom officers were holding the traditional first night party or RPC[4] on the quarterdeck immediately above our mess-deck. This RPC featured a brilliant steel band playing a few feet above the two scuttles or portholes in the mess. We of course were not invited to the RPC and so enjoyed the music, whilst fervently wishing we could join in and dance with the beautiful girls we had seen coming up the gangway. No chance.

However, some of us did get ashore on the second day and enjoyed the beaches and indeed a very memorable bar known as Harry's Bar which featured some entertainment as well as the usual Cuba Libre and other rum punches.

---

[4] The Navy does not use the term cocktail party but refers to such events by the ever-present acronym in the Services, in this case RPC, which translates as "Request the Pleasure of your Company".

British Guiana

Our visit to Barbados was to be cruelly abbreviated by an incident in British Guiana, some 350 miles to the South. At that time I had no idea where it was, what it was or what we were required to do. We were briefed that there were riots in this British Colony on the coast of South America, specifically in the capital, Georgetown. There were riots demonstrating against the Marxist-Leninist Chief Minister Mr Cheddi Jagan and his government and HMS WIZARD was to be dispatched, leaving the other three frigates to enjoy the beaches of Barbados.

As we steamed in to Georgetown, over a dangerous sand bar at the entrance, we could see enormous clouds of smoke over the port area. The Captain was in a hurry to berth but we were subjected to a reasonably strong wind blowing us off the jetty and several attempts by the forecastle seamen to get a heaving line ashore had failed dismally. The Captain leaning over the lip of the open bridge was encouraging, with some gusto, the fo'c'sle Petty Officer to do better.

While the seamen who had failed were recovering and recoiling their heaving-lines, ready for yet another attempt, I already had a heaving-line ready and suggested to the Petty Officer that I thought I could reach the jetty.

"Go on then, young Sir."

The line flew straight and true and the Guyanan on the jetty seemed suitably pleased when he trapped the heavy monkey's fist with a cleverly placed foot.

"How about that then PO?" I shouted with an enormous beam of satisfaction.

At that point I couldn't understand his complete lack of enthusiasm for my success.

"F-ing magic, young Sir. He's got one end of the line, but where is the other end?"

Needless to say, I had failed to remember to secure the inboard end to the guardrail.

We berthed a few moments later and several of us were then sent ashore with fire-fighting equipment to control the fires in the port warehouses. By 11 o'clock that evening I had wandered several hundred yards from the ship and after many hours of firefighting, was covered in a smoky residue so that I looked more like a Guyanan than a British Cadet. Seeing the red top light of the ship above a warehouse I approached, only to find my way barred by a wire fence.

I decided to climb the fence, rather than attempt to find my way round the warehouse. As I paused astride the fence with my back to the ship, I felt a sharp jab in my nether regions and a clear, bold Liverpudlian, "Alright – hold it there mate!" Having persuaded the Leading Seaman with the rifle that this blackened individual was indeed a Cadet from the WIZARD, I was allowed down.

The next day I was given a .303 rifle and one hundred rounds and told to stand sentry, alongside a seaman, on a crossroads in the capital to prevent looting and maintain law and order. As we chatted away that evening, the relative quiet was shattered by a sound, which I had a bit of trouble identifying. The seaman and I exchanged glances and the raised eyebrows as we realized we had been fired at and the sound was a round striking the road a few feet away. We soon spotted the bad guy, loitering unsteadily in a shop doorway about eighty yards away.

"What shall we do?" asked the seaman.

"Well if he fires again, I think we should let him know we are armed and should return fire," I replied.

"You're the officer, and I'll leave it to you then," replied the sailor.

We then warned the miscreant and told him to put the gun down, come out with his hands up and so on, but to absolutely no avail and he let another round off in our general direction. I had had enough and fired one round near his feet on the pavement. He gave up immediately. When our eight-hour watch completed, we returned to the ship and my troubles started.

"What do you mean, you have only got 99 rounds left?" barked the Chief GI.

"I shot someone," I replied.

"You what!" exploded the Chief

The exchange lasted for ages and that was only a start. It took about five pages of explanation as to why I had wasted a round.

After an exciting few months at sea it was back to Dartmouth for our final term and our passing-out parade inspected by Her Majesty the Queen.

Passing Out Parade, BRNC Dartmouth.
Yours truly is just about visible in the squad of cadets, behind the Midshipmen, in the second rank, four from the left and wearing glasses.

During the preparations for this important parade, which involved additional parade training at 0630, I recall the gunnery officer walking up and down the ranks inspecting our uniforms, webbing, haircut and general appearance. It was unusual for the gunnery officer himself to be involved at this unearthly hour of the morning and I was particularly surprised when he stopped in front of me, stared hard at my face and then leant down and under my chin.

"Did you shave this morning, Galloway?"

"Yes Sir," I replied.

"Then you need a new blade in your razor," he barked.

"Electric Sir," I retorted and immediately regretted the response.

"Well stand closer next time," he snarled and moved on.

1962/63 - MIDSHIPMAN'S YEAR

The flight to Singapore

The Murray 2 entry then went to join the fleet for a year at sea as midshipmen. Eight of us were to join HMS ARK ROYAL in Singapore and we set off in an RAF Bristol Britannia stopping off to refuel in Istanbul and Bombay. Unfortunately, the aircraft developed a fault in Bombay and we spent several hours waiting in the airport terminal while the RAF pondered the problem. The eight of us adjourned to the bar to await the outcome. Meanwhile the naval padre who had been nominated as the senior passenger on board, decided that that the mothers with very young babies, who were travelling to Singapore to join their husbands, were getting extremely tired as the evening drew on. The padre accordingly allocated one baby to each midshipman (yes there were eight babies) while the mothers had a two-hour rest. It seemed that the simplest way to accommodate the twin aims of looking after the babies and having a drink was to place the babies on the bar and carry on. The padre was not too amused but the mothers were very appreciative.

Later that evening it transpired that the aircraft was going nowhere for at least twelve hours and a decision was taken to take us all to hotels in Bombay. The drive through the streets of Bombay was another glimpse of life for those less fortunate, as we saw many thousands asleep on the wide pavements of the city. We dropped off the ladies with their babies, the senior officers and others, until the eight midshipmen remained. Our hotel was fine but limited in accommodation and we had to share.

I teamed up with a great friend, S, later to become a judge, and we prepared for the night. As he stripped off to take a shower, there was a knock on the door. Stark naked, he took refuge behind the door as I opened it a crack. Standing there was the extremely pretty RAF corporal from our flight who had come to tell us that our early morning call was at 0600 for a pickup at 0630. Meanwhile S, realizing that he was standing stark naked about two feet away from this pretty girl and separated only by a thin bit of wood, was trying to catch my eye to make me laugh. Furthermore, he started to make certain gestures, which could well have been misinterpreted by the corporal.

It was at this stage that I realized that while she continued to outline the arrangements for the morning, she wasn't really looking at me, but her gaze had shifted slightly to somewhere past my right ear. "Oh no," I thought, "surely not!" but my fears were confirmed as her smile disappeared, a dark glare developed and I turned to see what had distracted her. Sure enough, there was a full length mirror behind me and S, in all his glory, was still cavorting unaware of the damage caused. She stormed off muttering about our disgraceful behaviour. Needless to say, she wasn't very talkative on the rest of the flight to Singapore.

Six months in HMS ARK ROYAL

We joined the mighty ARK ROYAL on 6th August 1962, our home for the next six months. We were taken down to a large space beneath the quarterdeck, called the cabin flat and were impressed by the size of the cabins we could see leading off the flat, only to be told that we were to sling our hammocks between the various tin wardrobes and chests of drawers in the flat and that this was to be our communal cabin.

HMS ARK ROYAL Commissioned: February 1955, Scrapped 1980. Length: 804ft. Beam: 112ft. Draught: 10m. Displacement: 36,800tons (as built) 43,060 tons full load (1978) Complement: 2,250; 2640 Including Air staff.

Later, we were allocated two four-berth cabins right aft and just underneath the curved round down of the flight deck. Our initial sense of pleasure was soon tempered in the tropical heat of the Far East. Not only was the thick flight deck just a few inches above the top bunk an amazingly good heat radiator throughout the night, but also, the cabins were situated on the starboard quarter immediately beneath the spot on the flight deck where the WAFUs[5] tested the jet engines of the various aircraft when at sea. The noise, like the heat, was unbelievable.

On our first night in Singapore we were encouraged to visit the Officers Club in HMS TERROR at Sembawang. There were plenty of young, pretty girls at the club and it didn't take long for the eight of us to take to the dance floor by the pool. Unfortunately, we hadn't realized that the current dance-craze in the UK, the twist, had not reached the far-flung limits of the empire. The girls soon picked up the idea but the general harrumphing from the senior officers and wives of the daughters we were trying to influence with our imitations of drying your back with a towel, while stubbing out two cigarettes under your feet did not go down too well.

---

[5] Jack Speak: WAFU (Wet and flipping useless (other versions available!)) - General service name for the Fleet Air Arm, or anything to do with the FAA. Derived from Pusser's stores category of WAFU, referring to sleeveless, anti-static, and sheepskin-lined leather jerkins for issue only to Weapon And Fuel Users.

Perth, Australia

From Singapore we sailed south to Freemantle in Western Australia for a ship visit over several days. On the second day, seeing the enormous queue of people waiting to get on board to see around the ship, Cadet R and I decided that here was a great opportunity to find a couple of pretty girls to take to the wardroom ball and dinner on the Saturday at the end of the week. R said he would pick out the best couple as we strolled casually down the queue and we would simply ask them if they would like to jump the queue by coming with us up the officers' gangway.

It went to plan until he approached an extremely good-looking girl, without bothering to check out the friend and consequently I ended up with her Mum. On the day of the ball, R and I took a taxi to go and collect our partners. The door was answered by the mother, who though looking very attractive, was definitely not ready to go to the ball. However all was not lost as she explained that though she and her daughter had enjoyed our discomfort when we had met, they had taken pity and the daughter had arranged for her best friend to take Mum's place. We had a great evening.

Setting fire to a Royal Marine Major

From Singapore it was North to Hong Kong, then a British Crown Colony and we were immediately immersed in this strange land with vivid recollections of the recently released film *"The World of Suzie Wong"* featuring Nancy Kwan and William Holden. The Wan Chai district was as exciting and exotic as displayed in the film and we all swore we had seen Nancy Kwan on several occasions during our visit.

During a lunchtime RPC on the teak-decked quarterdeck of the carrier, I was with a group of young officers when the OCRM[6] Major joined us. A tall and imposing officer with, like most of us at the time, a penchant for the odd cigarette, I offered him one of mine and proceeded to flip my Zippo open and light it. He was considerably taller than me and as I went up, he came down and I missed the cigarette. His moustache, luxuriant to say the least, crackled into life as the flame discovered some fuel. Amidst the ripe language that accompanied the bonfire I had started, two thoughts flashed through my mind. Firstly; is this the end of my brief naval career – I have just set fire to a senior Royal Marine Officer; and secondly, how the hell do you extinguish a moustache?

Without a fire blanket to hand, my immediate thought turned to water but I was drinking a gin and tonic. Luckily, my glass was only half full and the tonic overcame the alcoholic content of the gin as I threw it at the Major and the moustache survived, albeit slightly smaller than before. The Major was surprisingly sanguine and carried on discussing the attractions of Hong Kong as though nothing had happened.

---

[6] Officer Commanding Royal Marines. We had a detachment on board, who apart from their normal RM duties manned one of the 4.5" RP 10 Twin Mark 2*** gun mountings on board.

The rugger match against the All Blacks

In Hong Kong we met up with the New Zealand frigate HMNZS TARANAKI, a converted Rothesay class frigate and a game of rugger was arranged. In ARK ROYAL we had a ship's complement of over two thousand, compared with two hundred and twenty in the TARANAKI, so we were fairly confident that we could field a good team and show the 'small ship' how the game should be played. I was selected to play as scrumhalf and we arrived at the pitch in good spirits. When the 'All Blacks' turned out, we realised that we might be facing a tougher game than we had expected. Many of the Maori players appeared to be as wide as they were tall and my opposite number looked particularly athletic as well.

The first five minutes were the best five minutes for ARK ROYAL and the remaining seventy-five minutes were very definitely slightly in favour of TARANAKI. Every time I managed to retrieve the ball from a scrum, it was as though someone dropped a large sack of flour on me, and the breath left my lungs, with amazing speed and regularity. The opposing scrumhalf always smiled as he helped me back to my feet, a gesture which I considered gentlemanly and sporting. The other sort of tackling, the ones where we were meant to tackle them, also posed a problem because the centre of gravity of many of the opposition was amazingly close to the turf and even if one did manage to grasp them around the thigh or calf, it didn't really seem to make any significant difference to their speed of advance.

At half-time we were knackered[7], and at full time, it was worse. After the match, we met up with the TARANAKI team in the bar and thrashed them when it came to beer consumption.

Oh yes. I forgot to mention the score in the other match – the rugger... 54 – Nil to them!

---

[7] A rugby term for completely buggered.

Revising for the Fleet Board

Towards the end of our time in the Far East the Training Officer, the Gunnery Officer, Lieutenant Commander F G S Walker RN, arranged that the eight midshipmen should be subjected to a mock midshipman's board in preparation for the real board at the end of our year at sea. We had been allocated a very small but comfortable compartment just for'd of the quarterdeck, known as the middies' gunroom and it was here that all eight of us were attempting to revise for this mock board on a very warm and humid afternoon. The chairs were comfortable and the climate had clearly got the better of us, as we were told later that all eight of us were sound asleep when the large frame of the Gunnery Officer filled the doorway.

"What DO you think you're doing?" thundered Guns.

I honestly can't remember which midshipman responded, but it was memorable.

'Well Sir, since it is only a mock board, we thought we would do some mock revision."

I cannot remember the punishment either but I don't think any of us went ashore for a few weeks.

A flight deck disaster

In the months we were in the Far East, we did suffer some very serious incidents on the flight deck, some resulting in fatalities. It is not appropriate to dwell on the accidents that resulted in the death of two our ship's company, but sufficient to say that both had occurred on the flight deck at sea and on successive alternate Saturdays. It was therefore with a certain amount of trepidation that we closed up for night flying exercises on the third successive such Saturday.

Everyone was aware that we needed to get through the evening without an incident of any kind and it had been decided to split the four hour flying exercise into two sessions with a change of watch of the flightdeck crew at the two hour point, thereby ensuring that concentration levels were as high as possible.

When we were under training with the Air department we were allocated duties on the flightdeck, which invariably required the least training and one of these was to act as a chock-man. Each aircraft on the flight deck would be assigned two chock-men when taxiing and when the aircraft reached its parking spot, the chocks would be placed either side of each main wheel. When aircraft landed they would taxi immediately to a temporary parking spot, Fly One, right forward on the starboard side, in front of the island. When all aircraft had been recovered, each aircraft would then turn and taxi down the flight deck on the starboard side until they reached the round down, right aft, and complete a full 180° turn, before taxiing up the port side to park, at a 30° angle facing to starboard, with the jet blast facing safely overboard to port.

This process was called the 'Elephant Tango' and was simple enough on a sunny, dry day when the ship motion was limited, but extraordinarily hairy when the sea conditions were rough, the stern might be rising and falling tens of feet and rolling several degrees when turning underway. If the weather was conspiring against you, the deck would be slippery and in the pitch darkness during the turn on the round down, life became interesting.

When a midshipman was allocated as a chock-man, the second chock-man, a member of the ship's company always ensured that the middy took the port wheel, thereby ensuring that during the Elephant Tango 180° turn, the middy would be running like hell, while he sat on his hunches laughing.

I had the first two-hour watch as a chock-man on that Saturday evening and assisted in parking a few aircraft, when, towards the end of my watch, I asked the Flight Deck Officer if I could witness the next series of landings, due to start after the watch change, from the Deck Landing Sight (DLS). Just as I was about to enter the DLS, the Petty Officer in charge of the chock-men, called me back to say that one of his team had been sent down to the sickbay with an injured hand and that he needed me for the landings to follow. I pointed out that I was due to go off watch in a few minutes, but he insisted that he needed me in case there was an unexpected emergency landing.

I never did get back to the DLS, because in the change of watch and an imminent landing, everyone was too busy closing up and handing over responsibility and it was agreed that my DLS experience would have to wait for another day.

When the watch changed, Warwick, the other midshipman in my watch, and I retired to our cabin, which we shared with the other six middies, right aft and just under the round down. There were only a few aircraft remaining in the air and we expected that flying operations would complete within about thirty minutes to an hour. Warwick and I, knowing that there was no chance of sleep until all aircraft were recovered, decided to watch the final landings from the gun sponson, right under the round down and immediately next to our cabin.

It was a beautifully clear and dark night and we watched as the first aircraft, a Sea Vixen, completed its turn towards the carrier, passing the destroyer acting as plane guard 3,000 yards astern, and approached on its pre-determined glide path. One could always tell if the pilot was 'on-the-ball', as indicated by the DLS, as the best pilots would need very little adjustment of their engine throttle to stay on the glide path and therefore land exactly correctly to catch one of the arrester wires. This position on the gun sponson was immediately beneath the centre of each aircraft as they passed overhead and the undercarriage and the tail hook would pass no more than twenty feet above our heads. The engine noise overhead was sensational and the crumph as the wheels hit the deck was equally impressive and one

MY BAGS ARE IN THE BACK

waited to hear the engine wind down if the aircraft had caught the wire, or indeed continue to full power if waved off.

The last few aircraft landed safely until the very last one who was waved off and did a bolter to go round again. As he approached, on his second attempt, we both agreed that he looked a bit low and was in fact almost exactly at our eye level instead of the normal 4° glide path. This was, to say the least, wrong and I turned to Warwick.

"I don't know about you," I said, "but I think it's time for a tactical withdrawal. Let's go."

I heard him say, "OK," and I turned to climb the two steps from the sponson up to the corridor outside our cabin. I had probably gone about fifteen feet when the most almighty crash, more like a detonation, filled the air and I hit the deck as deckhead insulation from above fell onto me. An immediate silence followed and I turned to see where Warwick was. Unbelievably, he was still standing on the sponson staring aft as though expecting another aircraft. When I got to him, he was clearly transfixed. After shaking him back into reality, he was more than surprised when I pointed out how close to disaster we had been. There had been a fifteen-foot length of cable three feet above the gun to hold an awning to protect it from the weather and this, together with the awning was no longer there. This was later found on the arrester hook of the Vixen. Warwick must be the only man alive to stand with his head five feet from the hook of a Vixen as it landed.

Meanwhile on the flightdeck, all hell had broken loose, because the Sea Vixen on impacting the rounddown had slewed to port and headed straight for the DLS, containing an officer and two ratings, one of whom was under training. The Sea Vixen, with a crew of two, crashed into the DLS and disappeared into the darkness over the side, taking the Sight with it. The question on everyone's mind was obvious. 'Had we just lost five men?'

The DLS, sometimes referred to as the Projector Sight, was situated on the port side, nearly abreast of the island, and did literally 'project', in that it was cantilevered over the ship's side, and the sea rushed by, sixty feet below. The crew manning the Sight were provided with a means of escape which involved jumping through a hole in the deck, into a canvas chute, which was constrained by rigging, in the shape of a curve, to dump the crew unceremoniously one deck below. I have often wondered whether, had the Petty Officer not called me back, I would have known where the chute was or more importantly whether all four of us would have had time to make it.

Initially, no one knew whether the Vixen crew had survived the crash and whether the DLS crew had managed to escape before the impact and the next few minutes were very tense. It soon transpired that the DLS crew had indeed all made it to the safety of the chute, but the third one down had missed the destruction of the Sight by milliseconds only and then we heard the brilliant news that the plane guard consort, steaming a few cables astern on the port side for night flying, had found the Vixen crew and rescued them both and they were safe and secure on board.

What a night and what a relief to have survived the third successive alternate Saturday without further loss of life.

A day in the main galley

As part of my training with the Supply department, I spent a day with the chefs in the main galley where they would produce three meals a day for two thousand in the ship's company and squadrons. I reported for duty at 0500 and was immediately asked if I could fry an egg. The affirmative reply was greeted with a smile and I was given several of the largest trays imaginable and told to prepare two thousand fried eggs for breakfast at 0630. After breakfast it was all hands to the pumps preparing for lunch. As I recall, there was an amazing selection of both hot and cold main courses, including beef, chicken, two pasta dishes, lamb, omelettes, several types of potato dishes and vegetables of every description together with various salads.

When I returned to the wardroom at 1345 for lunch, where one single place setting was still laid on the table, I asked what was on the menu, expecting a similar choice to the main galley for'd. The steward replied:

"Chicken, Sir."

"Nothing else?" I enquired. "No choices?"

"Oh yes, Sir. There is a choice. You can have it cold if you wait a while."

*

Our return to UK included a visit to another British Crown Colony, Aden, then down to Mombasa before heading North again to the Red Sea before entering the 87½ miles of the Suez Canal. We stopped off briefly at Gibraltar before returning to our homeport, Devonport.

P 1127 – The world's first deck landing

During my six months on board ARK ROYAL we carried out numerous flying exercises with the various embarked aircraft, including the Scimitar, Sea Vixen, Buccaneer, Gannet, Phantom and the Wessex helicopters but on 8th February 1963, we were privileged to see a world-first flying display. The flight deck had been cleared of everything, including the large rescue crane, to make the landing area less intimidating for the event to follow. We all knew what was intended but the next few minutes were truly amazing as the prototype Hawker Group's P1127 "jump-jet" arrived on station in the channel, accompanied by a meteor acting as chase plane.

The island was jam-packed with goofers as she made several passes at different speeds over the deck and then she approached on the same flight-path as a fixed wing aircraft and then, when about a cable astern, she started to slow down. As she passed over the round down she was travelling at about 40 knots, which was almost unbelievable, used as we were, to the normal 140-knot approach.

More, seemingly unbelievable, sights ensued as the pilot eased the jump-jet forward to the centre of the flight deck, slowed and very gently lowered to the deck. After a few seconds the 'plane rose to about twenty feet above the deck and then dipped and gently moved ahead, stopped and then, in a sight that no one on-board had ever seen before, she moved backwards. The sailors just loved it and as the cheering died away, a lone voice rang out above the whine of the jet engine, "Go on then, take it down the b....y hangar."

MY BAGS ARE IN THE BACK

8th February 1963. Hawker's Chief Test Pilot, Bill Bedford brings the P1127 jump-jet out to HMS ARK ROYAL in the channel for the world's first deck landing.

A week in HMS MARYTON, 17 - 22 Sep 1962

After some time in the Far East, the ARK ROYAL's Training Officer, probably needing a rest, sent us to a flotilla of Minesweepers operating in the area for a week. I joined the Ton Class Sweeper HMS MARYTON.

HMS MARYTON - Ton Class Minesweeper Launched: April 1958, Scrapped: July 1969, Length: 152ft. Beam: 28ft. Draught: 8ft. Displacement: 440 tons. Complement: 34.

A very unusual sign on the funnel

HMS MARYTON was in the 104th Minesweeping Squadron, and as I joined, I was struck by the sign, boldly displayed on both sides of her funnel, a black footprint within a red triangle.

It was, to say the least, unusual and I was intrigued as to what it was meant to convey. I asked a couple of young ratings I met but was not enlightened, apart from the fact that it was the Squadron sign. Later, I met the Engineering Mechanician and he was quick to explain that the sign owed its design to his engines. This did not convey the actual origins of the sign and I pushed for more information.

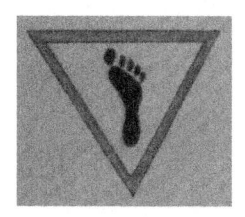

A sketch I made in 1963 of the Insignia on the funnel.

He continued to explain that the Ton Class Sweepers were propelled by Napier Deltic engines and hence the Greek delta symbol.

"What about the footprint, then?" I asked.

"That comes from the seamen and the First Lieutenant, the problem is that the deltic engine does produce a certain amount of soot, especially when we start up and the upper deck does get a gentle dusting of the oily deposit. In these warm climates, where the lads on the uppers tend to wander around in bare feet, they tend to leave a tell-tale trail of footprints. After one particularly bad day with the engines, the First Lieutenant lost his sense of humour as he was trying to get ready for Captain's rounds and was heard to utter the words which have since been embodied in the colour of the delta sign.

"What did he say?" I naively asked.

He grinned. "Bloody Deltics."

Sunset Ceremony – A total shambles

On the first evening on board MARYTON I found myself Officer of the Day at anchor close to the other four Sweepers.

As sunset approached, I took my place on the bridge wing to take the salute as two duty hands lowered the Ensign at the stern and the Jack on the jack staff. Well versed in the pomp and ceremony on the carrier, involving multiple officers, senior and junior ratings, a Royal Marine Band, a bugler and occasionally the four-ring Captain or even an Admiral, I found the informality on board the sweeper refreshing. However, I was not prepared for what followed.

As the exact time of sunset approached, I saw a small boat approaching from one of the other sweepers, accompanied by a pipe over the ship's broadcast that the "new films were arriving alongside". I found out later that it was definitely a case of first come, first served as far which mess got the best film. At this news, both of the Ratings manning the Ensign and Jack staffs, made a run for the ship's side to grab a film. I turned to the Leading Seaman on the bridge wing with me, to say that this was going to complicate the normally very precise ceremonial procedure, but he too had gone!

As the senior sweeper, HMS FISKERTON, one cable away, lowered the prep pennant and the sound of the 'still' on the bosun's call reached me across the water, I grabbed our call which our bosun's mate had left on the broadcast microphone, piped the still and made the announcement, "Sunset, attention on the upper deck, face aft and salute." Rushing down from the bridge, I lowered the Jack, ran aft and got the Ensign down, only to find the scrum around the film delivery totally unconcerned. Needless to say, the wardroom got last choice, or more accurately, the last film. The First Lieutenant was not amused and suggested I had displayed a serious lack of judgement.

The minesweeping exercise – Where's the Officer-of-the-Watch?

Later, we proceeded to sea for an overnight five-ship flotilla minesweeping exercise with each ship deploying sweep wires, otters, kites, floats and markers to both port and starboard, two hundred fathoms astern of each sweeper. Unsurprisingly I was told I had the middle watch on the bridge and I reported for duty at midnight. A very pleasant Sub-Lieutenant briefed me in the total darkness, pointing out the other sweepers, which seemed dangerously close and showed me the planned sweep we were to conduct for the next four hours. This involved a four mile leg, a 20 degree turn, followed by a two mile leg, all at 8 knots with each leg taking about 45 to 50 minutes.

"You may find the turns a bit tricky," he added. "You see we have to change lanes in a complicated manoeuvre, rather like a do-si-do in Scottish dancing. Did you do that at Dartmouth?" he enquired.

I replied that indeed I had, but failed to see the relevance.

"Any questions?" he asked.

"Only one," said I. "Where is the Officer of the Watch?"

"That's you lad," and he was gone.

In the ARK ROYAL, my duty on the bridge involved looking after the Captain's needs and very occasionally doing something vaguely important such as putting a fix on the chart, but here I was in command of one of Her Majesty's warships. I called down the voice-pipe to the quartermaster on the wheel, one deck below.

"Have you done this before QM?"

"Yes Sir, once, last year," he replied.

"I gather we will have to turn in about ten minutes and the Sub-Lieutenant suggested it might be a bit tricky. Any thoughts?" I asked.

"Don't worry Sir. You just look out the window and when they turn, give me the nod and I'll do the rest!"

I smiled at the ways of the little ships and started watching the senior officer's movements, a phrase which until then had meant something completely different.

Defaulters – The seaman, the cook and the fine.

During our midshipman's year at sea, we were detailed off to attend defaulters whenever and wherever they took place. In ARK ROYAL, defaulters were a grand affair, whether at the Commander's 'table' where the straightforward cases were dealt with, and the more serious cases referred up to the Captain's table. In the carrier the Captain's table involved a serious number of officers and ratings gathered around the table as the defaulter was marched in, whereas in MARYTON the occasion was more relaxed, albeit equally serious for the miscreant if found guilty and punishment was handed down.

During my week in MARYTON, Captain's defaulters were organised and I fell in alongside the court officers to witness and learn. The Captain of the sweeper was a young Lieutenant and he dealt with the first few offences with commendable skill and judgement. It was difficult to retain concentration in the heat of the Singapore morning and particularly since the charges were invariably 'absence from his place of duty' or 'did return on board one hour and three minutes late' and so on. However the scene changed radically as the next charge was read out for Able Seaman Ridley.

"Conduct prejudicial to good naval order and discipline in that he did return on board Her Majesty's Ship MARYTON at 2320 hours and did urinate upon the chef, Cook Simmonds, who was asleep on his camp-bed on the upper deck."

There was a very short pause as several of us composed ourselves and tried not to look around to see who was having trouble containing their barely concealed smiles. The Lieutenant, who would have known before the proceedings the exact wording of the charge, remained stony-faced.

"How do you plead?" enquired the Captain.

"Not guilty," replied Ridley.

The Coxswain then explained the facts of the case to the Captain and the rest of us wondered how Ridley and his representing counsel, in the form of his Divisional Officer, were intending to defend their case in view of the damning and straightforward evidence.

MY BAGS ARE IN THE BACK

"What have you got to say in response to this charge, Ridley?" said the Captain.

"Well Sir, I am pleading mitigation."

Eyebrows around the table rose as we took in Ridley's appreciation of the finer points of law, albeit mitigation was normally delivered just before sentence was passed.

The Captain looked Ridley in the eye. "Continue then, Ridley."

"I had been ashore with the lads and we'd had a few drinks and as you know it was really hot last night and several lads were trying to keep cool by sleeping on the upper deck. When I spotted Cook Simmonds turned in there, on his camp bed, and all comfortable like, I remembered the curry we had last night, so I decided to…"

The Captain interjected, "Yes, I think we know what happened next, thank you Ridley. Is there anything else you would like to add?"

"No, Sir. But I'd like to call a witness."

The case was getting progressively more and more intriguing and we noticed that this request caused even the Captain's eyebrows to rise. He indicated his approval and enquired as to whom Ridley would call, to help his cause.

Ridley didn't bat an eyelid. "I'd like to call Cook Simmonds please Sir."

At this, the case definitely took on a new slant and we were all very definitely intrigued as to where this was going to take us. Simmonds marched in and saluted and Ridley turned to him.

"Would you tell the Captain," said Ridley, "what you served for the ship's company meal last night."

"Curry, Sir," replied Simmonds.

"And would you tell the Captain what that curry was like," continued Ridley.

At this, Simmonds appeared to take a particularly deep breath and continued, "Well Sir, put it this way, Sir. It was really awful, terrible and ghastly. If I'd been ashore last night and returned and seen myself asleep and comfortable on my camp-bed on the upper deck, I'd have p****d on myself, just like Ridley did."

At this, it was almost impossible to contain oneself, but the Captain realising that the situation might well become farcical, pronounced, "I don't know how much money you have had to pay Simmonds, Ridley but I am certain it is far more than I am empowered to fine you. Case dismissed."

"On caps. Left turn. Quick march," barked the Coxswain and after a polite pause the Lieutenant turned away and we all broke down.

A week in HMS OTTER, 6 – 12 Jan 1963

In early January 1963 I was appointed to spend 6 days in the 'O' class submarine HMS OTTER, which had only been in commission for four months when I joined.

HMS OTTER (Oberon Class) Pennant Number: S15 Commissioned: August 1962, Scrapped: April 1992 Length: 295ft. Beam: 26ft. Draught: 18ft. Displacement: 2,140 tons full load submerged. Complement: 68 (6 officers, 62 ratings).

Based in Faslane, she was to conduct torpedo trials with a new Torpedo Control System in a nearby exercise area. The torpedoes, fitted with day-glow orange heads were fired down the range and it was relatively simple task to locate them and hand them over to the Torpedo recovery Vessels. However a few did go astray and the ship's company was then encouraged to look for them using any equipment and vantage point available. Binoculars and telescopes were deployed on the casing and the fin as we all tried to be first to spot the missing fish, not least because there was a tot of rum in it for the winner.

I decided that the additional height of the periscopes gave an obvious advantage and managed to grab one of them on several occasions and was accordingly lucky to spot three over the next few days, only to be told by the First lieutenant that Midshipmen were not entitled to have a tot. That was the end of that until the day I left the boat to travel back south to re-join the ARK ROYAL. With my bag packed, I was bidding farewell to the members of the wardroom, when the First Lieutenant presented me with a large glass containing three tots of rum and told me that since I was leaving they had decided that I was allowed to drink my reward.

When I awoke 24 hours later, I was informed that the wardroom had looked after me, after I passed out by putting me in one of the top bunks in the wardroom, while they had a mess party that evening with several local lasses, apparently, who were informed that I had been working so hard that I had not been to bed for three days, that I always went to bed in my civvy suit and that I always snored like that.

Unfortunately I was also 24 hours late returning to ARK ROYAL, but was allowed by the OTTER lot to say the submarine had been delayed on the trials by some really bad weather and that it had all been 'a bit of a rum do'! Hmmm!

Six months in HMS ESKIMO

Ship Handling

Having survived six months in an extremely large ship it was time for the eight of us to split up and sample life in a frigate. Two of us were appointed to the Tribal Class frigate, HMS ESKIMO which was so new that we joined her in the builder's shipyard, J Samuel White's, in the Isle of Wight.

HMS ESKIMO - Tribal Class Frigate
Commissioned: February 1963, Scrapped: 1992
Length: 360ft. Beam: 42ft. Draught: 17ft
Displacement; 2,700 tons full load. Complement: 253.

Two amazing things happened as we joined. Firstly, we experienced an amazing feat of seamanship by the new Commanding Officer, Commander J N Humphrey-Baker, as he handled the ship for the very first time and brought her across the Solent and into Portsmouth dockyard. He had been allocated a berth at North Wall, which required him to come in stern first. He turned down the offer of tug assistance with some disdain and came down the harbour half ahead at about 5 knots. Turning to port at the appropriate moment to swing away from the berth and line up the stern with the berth itself, he rang on "full astern" and we shot backwards. The only other two orders were "full ahead" and "finished with main engines" . This ship-handling was all the more remarkable because the Tribal Class frigates only had a single propeller and the consequent paddle-wheel affect at full speed ahead/astern is considerable, making steering, especially astern extremely difficult.

Safe-cracking

The next interesting moment on arrival on board concerns a cabin. It seemed unbelievable to the two newly arrived Midshipmen, but we were allocated a cabin each with all the space and fittings imaginable. Beneath the bunk was a metal drop-fronted desk, which contained a small metal combination safe for valuables. In went my passport, ID card, camera, wallet and so on and I swung the combination and explored the rest of this truly impressive cabin, a fantastic contrast to a hammock in a cabin flat. The other Midshipman, another Peter, and I decided to go ashore since we were not on duty that first night and I said I would be ready in half an hour.

It was of course at this stage that I realised I had not got a clue how to open the safe. No Instructions as to the default code of course, and there was no way I was going to admit to the Lieutenant, appointed as our training officer, that within 24 hours of joining I had locked all my valued possessions away in a safe that might require a locksmith to open it. After a bit of a discussion, I asked Peter to pop down to the sickbay and borrow a stethoscope while I took his identical safe to bits. We studied the mechanism and set about twirling the knob backwards and forwards on both safes, making copious notes as the recalcitrant safe emitted different sounds until, after about six hours, we cracked it.

Three men in a boat

When commissioning a new ship in those days, one task involved the calibration of the anti-submarine weapons, the Mortar Mk10. To ensure the minimization of ship movement during the calibration process, a special range was used off Portland, where the ship was moored between two buoys. The day dawned with a very stiff wind across the line of the buoys and we needed to attach anchor chain to both buoys. This involved taking one shackle[8] of anchor chain from for'd to aft before securing the bow to the first buoy with a short length of anchor chain, hauled in tight on the capstan and secured by a slip.

My involvement was to drive the boat, a three-in-one whaler, with two sailors on board, to attach the second shackle of anchor cable to the second buoy at the stern. The method was simple in theory and meant attaching a wire hawser to the buoy, which was then hauled in, by winch, by the hands on the quarterdeck. When the buoy was hauled in close enough to the ship, we would be able to take the anchor chain, hanging from the frigate's stern, and attach it the second buoy, using an enormous and heavy anchor shackle.

The buoy-jumper, the sailor who had drawn the short straw, would then jump from the whaler onto the buoy, attach the anchor cable with the shackle and then we could all get back on board the frigate. The wind had other ideas. Every time we tried to put the jumper on the buoy, the wind would gust, the frigate would be blown several yards downwind and of course the buoy would slowly submerge. At this point, we would recover the jumper who was floating dangerously close to the transom of the 2,500 ton frigate and treading water somewhere above a massive buoy, waiting to pop up somewhere nearby.

It was March and apart from the bitter wind, it was raining and we were incredibly cold, especially the jumper, but we had a deadline to meet, to vacate the range by mid-afternoon, so we had to persevere. On about the sixth attempt and about three hours later, we were secured and we returned to the falls to be hauled on board. The

---

[8] One shackle is 15 fathoms, 90 feet or 27.432 metres.

Captain decided that apart from some warm dry clothes, we should be rewarded with a tot of rum or two. "Here we go again!" I thought, but I must admit that the tot really did the trick and I still recall the medical miracle as it warmed me from within.

Sailing close to the wind

When I left the ship I was interviewed by the Commanding Officer, Commander Humphrey-Baker who took me through my "end-of-term" report, the form S206, but first he said how very pleased he was with the way I had handled the missing bottle of scotch. I had completely forgotten that when I had joined and been tasked with the duty of wardroom wine caterer, I had, within one week, 'lost' a complete bottle of whisky. I decided to lose a tot every day until I could balance the books. I never did find out who lifted the bottle.

After a very reasonable report, he let me out of his cabin with the following phrase ringing in my ears, "I don't think I've ever served with a young officer who sails so close to the wind, without going about."

1963-1967 - ROYAL NAVAL ENGINEERING COLLEGE (RNEC)

Engineering training for officers in those days meant attending the RNEC at Manadon on the outskirts of Plymouth, where one undertook either a BSc or an HND course. I was assessed as possibly bright enough to get a degree and the next three years proved how marginal that decision was. I failed the final year of my degree, together with seventeen out of thirty-four of my specialization. We, the unsuccessful students, blamed the way some of our instructors had failed to deliver a broad enough coverage of the London University external degree syllabus. Whoever was to blame for this unbelievably poor performance, the good news was that some, but not all, of the seventeen were allowed to 'go round again'.

Dirty deeds in my 1938 MG TA

I joined the college in September 1963 and within weeks had met and fallen violently in love with an extremely beautiful girl who lived, with her mother, on the Hoe, overlooking Plymouth Sound. Her father had unfortunately died when she was only six, following an exciting naval career in the Second World War involved in thirty-eight convoys in HMS WELLINGTON, mostly in the Atlantic and then incredibly hazardous convoys to Russia and to Malta in HMS ICARUS. I mention this because it soon became clear that her mother did not appear to mind me paying particular attention to her daughter. Perhaps it was the uniform.

One day soon after we had met, I asked her mother if I could take her daughter to the ball at BRNC Dartmouth, where one of my younger cousins was undergoing training. Her mother considered my request, asked when the ball would end and when I told her carriages were at one, she agreed as long as we were back by two. "No problem," I replied.

Came the day and I picked up my date in my 1938 MG TA and couldn't really understand why I was asked to put the hood up for the thirty-two mile trip, but was informed it was a matter of hairstyle preservation. The ball was an outstanding success and I remember ending up with a group of officers and girlfriends in the splendour of the Captain's house with the Captain's daughter encouraging us to do some damage to her father's drinks cabinet. As the time for departure approached, the Captain's daughter suggested that we should all drive over to Torquay, go to the bowling alley for a few games and then we would get a free breakfast if we were still there at four-thirty in the morning. What a great idea we all thought and off we went.

After breakfast, at about six-thirty as we approached Plymouth, I realized I was in really serious trouble. I stopped the car about one hundred yards around the corner from her mother's house, removed my mess jacket, rolled my shirt sleeves up and opened the bonnet. It wasn't difficult to find some grease and a suitable amount was used to anoint my forehead, arms and hands. Motoring the last few yards to the house, I was suitably alarmed to find her mother staring out of the sitting-room window. I felt awful as we entered the house and was about to deliver the most humble apology when her mother took over.

"Oh dear," she said, "I knew something awful must have happened when you didn't make it back on time and I guessed that your old car had let you down. Look at the state of you. I'll go and run a bath and then you must be hungry, so I'll get some bacon and eggs ready."

It seemed a pity and rather churlish to dissuade her and I didn't tell her the whole story until thirty-one years later, which was thirty years after I had married her daughter.

The run ashore and the police sergeant

A great friend of mine at RNEC, John, also owned an MG, a 1939 TB Tickford, almost identical to the TA except that the two doors were not cut away to elbow height and this gave the car a certain stylish elegance. John and I had shared many good times in our two sports cars but there was one particular night when it all went astray. A group of us had spent a couple of hours in a few of the pubs on Dartmoor such as "The Who'd Have Thought It", "The Skylark" and the "Royal Oak" and then John and I together with one passenger each decided to round off the evening in The Sailing Club on the Barbican in Plymouth. Leaving there at about 11pm, John and I decided to see who could get back to the College first. About half way back there is a short 300yd stretch of dual carriageway up a hill just North of Mutley Plain.

The two MGs were almost abreast up the hill, with John having the edge and just drawing past me, when his engine spluttered as he ran out of fuel. I smiled as we sped on but then heard his engine roar back to life as he flicked the dashboard switch to change to the reserve tank. By this time, we were well ahead and approaching the slight left bend at the top of the rise and the subsequent right bend. As we rounded the right-hand bend at some considerable speed, there on the pavement was a police constable who evidently could hear or see the TB behind us and was intent on stepping into the road to stop it. I checked my mirror to see if John had managed to miss him and was surprised to see red lights that quickly changed to white. The TB was pirouetting in the road right in front of the constable. I turned to my passenger.

"Stop or go?" I enquired. "Keep going, there's no point in both of you getting booked."

We pulled in a few hundred yards down from the incident and walked back to the TB now 'parked' on the grass verge a bit too close to a 'Blind Persons Crossing' sign and with a very badly buckled wheel, damaged in mounting the considerable kerb. The police constable had already produced his notebook and was licking the end of his pencil as we strode up. At that moment a police Ford Zephyr came roaring up from Plymouth and drew up alongside. The police sergeant who emerged looked at the four naval officers.

"You were travelling then. We've been trying to catch you since the city-centre. Manadon I suppose, is it?"

Then turning to the constable, he continued, "You're a lucky lad then. You don't see many of these TBs around these days. You can put your pencil away."

"But Sarge," spluttered the constable, "they were both doing well over 50 'round that corner and it's a 30 mph limit."

"I'm sure you're right constable but these cars are very precious and valuable, so put your notebook away, get your sleeves rolled up and help the young officer to change that buckled wheel."

"I see you've sprung a radiator leak too, Sir," continued the Sergeant. "I think you are going to need a tow back to the College and I don't suppose the other MG will manage to tow you up that last hill to Manadon, so we'll do it."

Turning to me, he enquired, "And what are you driving Sir?"

"A '38 TA," I replied.

"Amazing. It doesn't get better than this, does it constable?"

The constable appeared not to hear this and continued to help changing the wheel. Turning to his driver the Sergeant continued: "Well don't just stand there, get the tow rope out. Look lively. These lads need to get some rest."

*

Months later, while driving back from Dartmoor one night, a Dartmoor pony leapt from the darkness onto the bonnet of the MG causing extensive damage. I rebuilt the car and when the 'extremely beautiful daughter', Lynn, agreed to marry me, we drove away from the wedding to our honeymoon. However, it soon became clear that an old MG was not the ideal vehicle in which Lynn was going to learn to drive and we sold her, the car that is and not Lynn, to a Metropolitan policeman for the princely sum of £120[9], which was £20 more than I had paid for it.

---

[9] Exactly fifty years later, I discovered 'my' MG had been completely restored and was on sale 20 miles from my home in Gosport for £29,500.

The MG TA after the rebuild.

1969-1971 - HMS HAMPSHIRE

A one week joining routine

I was supposed to fly from Heathrow to join the County Class destroyer, HMS HAMPSHIRE, in Barbados, an island that I had visited, albeit briefly in 1962.

Our flight involved a change of 'plane in New York but at about the halfway point across the Atlantic, we were informed that a blizzard in New York had closed the runway and we would be diverting to Montreal. Having expected to step off the second plane from New York, into the Caribbean warmth, it was one enormous shock to walk down the steps in Montreal in a short-sleeved shirt and experience temperatures below freezing as we walked the three hundred yards, through the darkness, to the terminal. Unsurprisingly, there were an awful lot of diverted flights at the airport and everywhere was jam-packed solid.

Having spent a while on the flight talking to the passenger next to me who was intending to establish his own property development company in the West Indies, it seemed natural for us to continue the conversation in the airport bar, while the authorities decided how to get us all to New York. After an hour and a few gin and tonics, we were informed that we would be staying in hotels overnight and getting to New York by coach in the morning.

HMS HAMPSHIRE - County Class Destroyer
Commissioned: March 1963, Sold for scrap: 1979
Length: 521 ft. Beam: 54ft. Draught: 20ft.
Displacement: 6,800 tons. Complement: 471.

In the late '60s there were no such things as credit cards and cash was the order of the day as we asked for the bill, which I had presumed we would be splitting. At this point in the story, I should add that I had begun to doubt the ambition of this relatively young entrepreneur, partly because his mention of several deals he had on the back burner sounded a bit fanciful, but who was I to cast judgment.

The bill arrived and I just could not believe the amount. At first I thought the bill was for every single passenger on our flight. It was something like ten times what I had envisaged and there was no way I had enough cash to pay my half.

"Let's have a look then," said my fellow passenger, "that seems pretty reasonable for an airport. I'll get this," he continued as he rolled off some notes.

I was so very ashamed to think that I had assumed that he had been bragging a few moments before.

This was only the first problem I was to face concerning a

shortage of money as I tried to join my ship.

After a night in Montreal, we travelled through the snow to New York and were accommodated in another hotel, since the runways were still closed. By now I definitely needed some warmer clothes, not to mention some washing and shaving kit, but our luggage was nowhere to be found. I needed some funds. Since I was travelling on a NATO travel order, I took a cab to the United Nations, explained my predicament and within a few seconds, was asked, "How much do you want?"

"Could you manage $100?" I asked, rather timidly.

"Anything you say," and I was outside with a wallet full of dollars, a few moments later.

We remained snow-bound in New York for a further four days and I was then informed that the ship had left Barbados and I was to wait for flight details as and when they became known. Eventually, I was told to make my way to the West Terminal by cab for a flight to Panama. The snow was piled several feet high on the sidewalks and one had to hail a cab by finding a gap in the snow wall. After a while I was lucky, got in with my recently returned luggage and asked to go to the West Terminal.

"You're going the wrong way!" drawled the cabbie.

I wondered how he could possibly know where I was going and why West Terminal was the 'wrong way'.

"No," I replied, "I definitely need to get to West Terminal."

"Are you a Limey or something?" sneered the cabbie. "This cab is facing East and if you want to go West, you need a cab facing the other way."

I couldn't believe he wanted me to get my luggage out, trek across the icy street and hail another cab, especially having spent about twenty minutes waiting for this particular one.

"I'll tell you what," said I, "I'll make it worth your while if you turn round and get me to West Terminal."

"OK fine, just this time," he replied as we turned and sped away.

Needless to say, it was most certainly not worth his while when we arrived at the Terminal and I don't think he will ever speak to me again.

Six days after leaving UK, I was bound for Panama in a large but almost deserted passenger airliner. I decided to celebrate and asked for a gin and tonic. The charming Air Hostess went aft and produced the drink. Some time later, with no one to talk to, I decided on another and she repeated the service. I noticed that when I asked for the third gin, she gave me a quizzical look and went to the front of the plane for a couple of minutes, before walking past me to the rear with a nice smile and a polite, "Won't be a minute Sir."

When the gin arrived, she apologized for the delay by explaining that she was worried that I might be a nervous passenger trying to summon up some Dutch courage before doing something foolish.

"How did you decide that I wasn't?" I enquired.

"That was easy," she said, "I just checked the passenger list with the head steward who told me you were a naval officer and that all naval officers drink like that."

We arrived in Panama, only to find that HAMPSHIRE was delayed, having suffered a technical problem on the way and I would have to spend another night in a hotel and off I went.

The next day was 14th February and I decided I would surprise my wife, who was expecting a child in a month's time, by telephoning her and wishing her a Happy Valentine's day. I was more than slightly surprised when my mother-in-law, who lived 180 miles from our house, answered the phone.

"Isn't it just wonderful?" she gushed, "Everything is fine and we are so excited," and on she went. I had absolutely no idea what she was talking about.

"What are we celebrating?" I said over the phone from Panama.

"Didn't you get my telegram?"

"No, I don't know what you're talking about," I replied.

"I sent a telegram to the ship yesterday. You must have got it. All the details about the baby. Isn't it marvellous?"

Eventually the realization hit me. My mother-in-law was in my house, because Lynn had produced our child one month earlier than planned and she thought I was on board HAMPSHIRE and had received the telegram.

I managed to get the basic facts from her. A boy, healthy and there were no complications.

Alone in my hotel room, I did what all film stars did and sent down for a bottle of scotch. When the waiter arrived, a Panamanian called Fernando, I asked him to get a second glass from the bathroom and join me in celebrating the birth of our son, Justin. I knew he was to be called Justin, because Lynn and I, not knowing the sex of our child before he or she was born, had agreed on a name for a boy or a girl. I found out several months later when I got home that Lynn could not work out how she had got a letter from me on the day when Justin was born, congratulating her and asking her to look after Justin until I first saw him. What I had done, of course was to leave two letters with a neighbour and entrust him to deliver the appropriate one at the right time.

Fernando and I finished the scotch and he went his way. Later I went down to lunch and found out that HAMPSHIRE was due to arrive in the morning. I wanted to thank Fernando for helping me celebrate the birth and asked at Reception where I might find him.

"Oh he's been sacked for being drunk," said the receptionist.

I sought out the manager and explained that my son had just been born and that Fernando was helping me to celebrate at my specific request. I implored him to re-instate Fernando and he undertook to consider it. I am glad to say that Fernando was serving at breakfast the next day.

HMS HAMPSHIRE duly arrived the next morning at ten o'clock and I reported on board seven days after leaving Heathrow. The wardroom was alive with about forty officers in their whites, drinking champagne. I introduced myself to one group and asked what the celebration was in aid of.

"Oh someone's had a baby," said a Lieutenant.

"That's a coincidence," I said. "So have I."

"What's your name?" said the Lieutenant.

"Galloway."

"It's yours."

The wardroom had opened the telegram and the bar and decided to celebrate my news. I was faced with a mess bill equivalent to one month's pay before I even joined the ship. It was also a sign of the times to come in a very fun-loving ship, known by us all as the "Happy HAMPSHIRE".

A 'phone call home from Cape Horn

There were no satellite telephone facilities in the late 60s and the only way to contact home was by radiotelephone to Portishead. It was planned that the ship would book a slot for a radiotelephone calls as we rounded Cape Horn and I was as keen as anyone of the five hundred men on board to make a call home. The lucky few were allowed two minutes each and the system operated in a simplex manner, meaning that one person could speak and end with "over" and release the transmit button. Our two-minute conversation went something like: "Hello darling. Listen carefully. When I say 'over' it is your turn to talk. When you finish, you must say 'over'. Over."

"Who's that? Over."

"It's me. Peter. Over."

"Hello darling, is that really you darling? Over."

"Yes, it really is me. I can't believe it's you. Over."

"How are you darling? Over."

"I'm fine. How are you? Over."

"I'm fine. How are you darling? Over."

"I'm fine. How is our son? Over."

"He's fine. Where are you darling? Over."

"Cape Horn darling. Over."

"Don't be silly darling, where are you? Over."

At this point, a different voice came on the line.

"Time's up caller."

It was to be another three months until I saw my son.

1971/72 - SOUTHAMPTON UNIVERSITY - MSC

The sparking plug, the bus stop and the pensioner

In the early seventies, the Navy was developing digital fire control systems for gunnery to replace the antique analogue systems. There was a requirement for an officer to join the team at the Admiralty Surface Weapons Establishment on Portsdown hill above Portsmouth, but there was no one available with the right technical background of digital filtering. I was lucky enough to be selected to attend Southampton University to study for an MSc in Electronics with a dissertation tackling the innovative subject of the Kalman Filter, a means of digital filtering, or iterative processing, to optimize processes.

At the time we were living in married quarters in Portsmouth and I decided to commute by motorbike each day for the one-year course. The bike was a single cylinder, 160cc Ducati. One day, while coming home, I was just leaving the 30 mph limit near Southampton and decided to give the bike a bit of throttle as I approached a gentle uphill section of the A27. As I passed a bus stop on my left, which had a large glass rear panel to protect waiting passengers, three things happened at once. The bike lost all power, the vast glass sheet shattered and the single male pensioner waiting for a bus fell to the ground.

Forgetting about my bike's, hopefully temporary, loss of power, I pulled over, rested the bike on its stand and rushed to help the pensioner.

"Are you all right?" I enquired as I helped him to his feet and sat him down on the bus shelter seat.

"I am a bit shaken," he admitted. "I am not sure what happened. I remember you passing and then the bus shelter sort of exploded."

At this we both turned to look at the glass, which had shattered and now lay in a reasonably tidy pile on the pavement. It was then that I wondered why there should be a smoking spark plug amongst the debris.

"Oh no," I thought. Loss of power. Shattered glass. Pensioner falls over. Smoking spark plug.

Still wearing my motorbike gloves, I leant down, recovered the plug and palmed it until it cooled enough to pocket it. After a few minutes reassuring the gentleman and checking he was unharmed, he thanked me and suggested I should carry on with my journey home, as his bus was due at any moment. I walked back to the bike, bent down to check whether the spark plug was indeed missing. The plug on this particular bike was angled at 45deg on the nearside and the plug was definitely missing, so there was absolutely no doubt about what had happened.

I recovered the plug from my pocket and covertly screwed it back in, tightening it by hand and was surprised to fine the thread held. I mounted the bike, made sure the spark plug was not pointing in a "dangerous direction" , held my breath and kicked started it. As the engine started, I turned to wave the pensioner, whose bus was coincidentally arriving at the stop, waved and decided to wait until the bus passed me in case the additional load as I accelerated, ejected the plug and destroyed something else. All was well and I got home and later fitted a thread insert and completed the course.

The card reader and the printout

My MSc involved both an examination and a dissertation and the latter involved the study of the accuracy of radar systems used in naval gunnery and to do this I obtained some data on the radar tracks of aeroplanes landing at airports. Whilst radar systems would track the 'centre' of an approaching target, this would only be true for an aeroplane at a distance, but as the plane got closer the system might, and indeed would, transfer its point of interest to 'alternative' targets and on a plane, these alternatives were the main engines or indeed the wings or even the wing tips.

The Kalman Filter used an optimization process, involving the best estimate of a variable by updating a previous best estimate, in accordance with the equations of motion. This involved some highly complex equations and recursive algorithms working on the variance of the errors involved. For three months, I ran a program that varied the parameters of the Filter to optimize the system and minimize the tracking error. This program was so complex that the computing department at the University would only allow me to run the program overnight. Each run of the computer only produced one page of output on the continuous form stationery, measuring 15in x 11in. This was a pictorial representation of the raw tracking data, the optimized track, the errors and various other parameters, but in essence showed the aircraft approaching the airport from twelve miles out until touchdown. Each morning I would return to University, collect my single sheet of computer printout and analyse the results.

In those days, the mainframe computer programs were on printed cards and my program was on about two hundred cards and adjusting the various parameters in the tracking algorithm, involved changing the data on just one or two cards. Day after day I repeated the process and there was no doubt that the optimization process was getting fantastic results and my tutor and I decided that the time had come to improve the size of the output, the single page of computer printout. We thought that two pages of output would enable us to inspect the results more accurately and so I adjusted the computer card that set the dimensions of the Y-axis.

The next morning, as I collected my expected output of two pages from the computer department, the normal envelope was missing from my pigeonhole. Going across to computer reception, I asked if there had been an overnight problem with the computer.

"No, no problem with the system," came the reply. "But you have got one helluva printout. It's over there," he said, pointing to a trolley containing stacks and stacks of the folded continuous form computer printout. If stacked on top of each other the printout would have measured five or six feet high. Later, I found out that this one printout had used one month's normal printout consumption for the entire university. When I looked at the card containing the new dimension on the Y-axis, I found it was in kilometres instead of millimetres, a multiplication factor of 10^6.

The MSc was eventually conferred and my professor wanted me to stay on, working for a PhD using my Digital Filtering experience to assist him with his work on closed-loop control systems in artificial limbs. I leaped at the opportunity but the RN had other ideas that the experience I had gained would be better employed in digital fire control systems. Funny that.

1972 – 1974 - ADMIRALTY SURFACE WEAPONS ESTABLISHMENT (ASWE)

Perched on the western end of the South Downs and overlooking Portsmouth, stands the imposing establishment, responsible for research into advanced technological systems for the Royal Navy. The Admiralty Surface Weapons Establishment originated in an Experimental Department set up in 1917 at HM Signal School, Portsmouth, to coordinate research work undertaken since 1896 on the Torpedo School ships, HMS Defiance and HMS Vernon. In 1941 the Experimental Department became the Admiralty Signal Establishment, which, like its predecessors, was largely concerned with communications. However, technological advances during the Second World War necessitated an increase in related fields of research, and in 1948 these were brought under one body, the Admiralty Signal and Radar Establishment[10] at Portsmouth.

In 1959 it was decided that missile technology justified an extension of its scope, and on being amalgamated with the Admiralty Gunnery Establishment (AGE) it received the title of Admiralty Surface Weapons Establishment (ASWE). It is responsible for various aspects of research, development, design and trial of equipment, devices and techniques in the fields of communications, radar missile control, and electronic counter-measures and in related fields. In 1971 the Admiralty Compass Observatory was absorbed

---

[10] Rumour has it, that in fact it was originally termed the Admiralty Radar and Signals Establishment but someone nearby objected to the local road-signs, using the four-letter acronym.

into ASWE as its Navigation Division, and in 1984 the Establishment was amalgamated with Admiralty Underwater Weapons Establishment (AUWE) and Admiralty Marine Technology Establishment (AMTE) to form the Admiralty Research Establishment (ARE).

A Lieutenant docks a destroyer

I spent nearly three years helping to develop the Royal Navy's first digital fire control system for gunnery. It was termed the Gun System Automation Mk 1 (GSA 1) and was going to be trialled in the Type 82 destroyer HMS BRISTOL, under construction at Swan Hunter & Tyne Shipbuilders at Wallsend. Whilst the software was an extremely important part of the new system, the hardware was also novel and involved the integration and alignment of six critical components in BRISTOL. My Project Leader at ASWE asked me to take on this aspect and it was not long before I found that things were not quite right at Wallsend.

In gunnery systems, when attempting to engage aircraft or missiles at ranges of several miles, the time of flight of the shell is many seconds and of course the target has moved an enormous distance in that time. An error of 1/3600th of a degree, or one second, of arc will cause a miss of one foot at 1000yd and every effort is therefore made to minimise all alignment errors in both the training and elevation planes. All systems in warships are aligned to two datum plates, in training and elevation, low down near the keel, in the longitudinal centre of the ship and very close to the gyrocompass.

When I checked the alignment of the two main fire control radars, the Lookout Aiming Sights (LAS) and the gun, I was initially pleased to find that the radars and the gun had been installed within specification and that any residual error could be readily corrected by software. The LAS however were displaying results, which varied every time we checked them. It transpired that the LAS had been installed on decking which was moving with the ship motion. The ship was bending and strengthening was needed beneath the LAS.

Much more worryingly, when carrying out a basic alignment check involving telescopes in the gun barrel and others on the radars, I had no trouble looking through the gun telescope to see the static target some miles away on one radar, but absolutely no chance of even seeing the target, let alone to the correct accuracy on the other. I checked our figures from previous alignment checks and there it was. The two systems were aligned within less than one minute of arc. How could it be then that we could not see the target? We were so used to working in seconds of arc that no one had bothered to check the degrees. The radar had been welded down exactly one degree out of alignment in elevation.

At this point, we needed to put this 7000-ton warship back into dry dock, secure her accurately and repeat some tests to establish the alignment problem and make the necessary corrections. This lengthy procedure was going to delay the ship's acceptance trials and the senior four-ringed Captain, recently appointed, was, to say the least unconvinced that this young Lieutenant had the faintest idea of what he was doing or of the ramifications for his command and career.

I was called to his cabin and spent nearly an hour convincing him that I did know what I was talking about.

'If you are wrong," he said, "I am going to make sure you are never allowed near another ship under construction again," or something like that.

We docked, corrected the problems and some months later carried out the first firing trial. Normally one might expect to obtain figures of anything between 0 and 90%, when engaging an aerial towed target and it was with some trepidation that we set out on our first firing run. No navy in the world had ever attempted to control a gunnery system digitally. We fired fourteen rounds and obtained thirteen bursts or hits, with the fourteenth bursting early, which sometimes occurred anyway, and which did not reflect on the accuracy of the gunnery system at all. The Captain spoke to me again.

The immigration problem at Heathrow

The trials progressed well and the Project team spent many days at sea in HMS BRISTOL conducting a variety of firings in the various surface and anti-aircraft modes. On one occasion we had completed the trials and were due to return to Portsmouth when it was announced on the ship's main broadcast that the ship was diverting to provide assistance to a vessel near the French coast. Later that evening it was decided that BRISTOL would spend the night in the French port of Dunkirk and the Project team would fly back to Heathrow.

I told my Project Leader, a Commander who had recently joined the team, that I did not have my passport and I hoped that this was not going to pose a problem. We agreed that if the French authorities allowed me to board the 'plane, I would probably be able to talk my way through the UK immigration authorities. At the airport, the French could not understand how I could be in France and not carrying a passport and they assured me that I would face all sorts of problems at Heathrow. If, however, I was prepared to take the risk, they in turn were prepared to let me go. We left France.

On arrival at Heathrow, I admit I approached the immigration desk with some trepidation, since the only means of identification I possessed was my RN Identification Card. I turned to my Project Leader, the Commander, who was immediately behind me.

"I trust you will vouch for me, if there's any trouble, Sir," I said.

"You're on your own Lieutenant," he replied, with an enormous grin.

With this in mind, I approached the desk and the immigration officer looked at my ID card, almost saluted me and without further ado, smiled and said, "Welcome home, Sir."

At this and bearing in mind the Commander's big grin and the fact that he had been born in Bangladesh and although totally Anglicized in every respect, he did have a darkish skin, I whispered to the Immigration Officer that the 'chap behind me' had been acting rather oddly on the plane and was perhaps worth a careful check.

I was in stitches as he was questioned and although he was through in a couple of minutes, it was sweet revenge. I bought him a drink later and we became and remained good friends for many years.

An offer to become a Polaris Systems Officer

The most senior RN officer at ASWE was a Commodore, who I certainly had not met during my time there, and I was certainly surprised to receive a summons from his secretary, one Friday afternoon. I approached his office with some trepidation, wondering what had gone wrong and indeed whether this was a reflection on my performance in HMS BRISTOL and the way the Commanding officer had reacted. However, as I was shown in to his office, I was immediately reassured when the Commodore indicated that I should take a seat in a very large leather armchair and then he asked his secretary to provide tea for both of us. I was, to say the least, perplexed.

"I have been watching your progress and performance here with considerable interest," he started. "And I have decided that you have considerable potential and I have decided to take a personal interest in your career."

I sat forward in my seat, wondering where this was going, when he continued, "To that end, I am going to suggest to the Naval Secretary that you should proceed, after this appointment, to a university of your choice to obtain an MSc."

"But Sir," I interjected.

He held up his hand. "No don't interrupt, Peter."

First names now, I thought and tried again, "But, Sir."

"Not now, Peter. Let me finish," he retorted. "I want you to go and get an MSc and then I will make sure that you can join the elite, as a Polaris Systems Officer, or PSO, as we say."

I tried again to interrupt, but again he dismissed my attempts and I gave in to this officer, four ranks above me in the naval hierarchy.

"I want you to go home for the weekend," he continued. "And give this amazing offer some very careful consideration and then come and see me first thing on Monday at, say, 0830. I will keep my diary clear and look forward to a minor celebration as we set you off on an exciting first step in your illustrious career."

"Well thank you very much indeed Sir," I replied. "But could I, first of all…"

"Not now, Peter," he chipped in. "I don't want another word about this until Monday when you have had time to consider this golden opportunity. OK?"

I was shown to the door and I left basking in the thought that I had been chosen for such personal interest from such a senior officer. At home, my wife and I investigated what being a Polaris Systems Officer might involve and spent many an hour deciding on this important decision.

Monday morning came round quickly and I reported to the Commodore as requested and was immediately shown to the same, very comfortable armchair.

"Well Peter," he said, with a big smile. "Are we all agreed on the plan then?"

"Before we start, Sir," I chipped in, "can we clear up one little detail."

"Of course. What's on your mind?"

"Well, you see Sir," I replied, almost apologetically, "I already have an MSc."

The Commodore's smile got even wider.

"That's brilliant then. We've just saved a year. Marvellous."

He then picked up a clipboard, scribbled some notes, looked rather thunderous as he mumbled something that sounded something like; 'bloody staff – can't trust them to get anything right these days.'

Looking up, he re-affixed his smile and continued, "Well, after that excellent news, that just leaves your decision on the PSO job."

"Yes Sir," I replied, and I think he had already detected some diffidence by virtue of the tone of my opening two words.

"I have given this the careful consideration you suggested, and I…"

"Yes Peter," he asked quizzically, leaning forward.

"Well, Sir. I don't think it is for me at all."

I was out of the office in less than ten seconds with a terse 'Too bad' from the Commodore.

As I walked away, I heard him calling to his secretary.

"Cancel the tea for two and get the next one up here will you, and be damned sure you find out whether or not they have already got an MSc."

1975-1977 - HMS ACHILLES

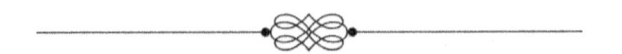

The Hong Kong dinner jacket

I joined HMS ACHILLES in Hong Kong as the Weapon Engineer officer and as a Head of Department and as a newly promoted Lieutenant Commander, I was entitled to a single cabin. The cabin was one of four, of similar size, located around an open space known as the cabin flat. When alongside, this cabin flat was often made available to various traders who would be invited to set up shop and sell their wares. In somewhere like Hong Kong, the likely traders would include tailors, cobblers or general merchants selling everything from paper umbrellas to cameras.

On my very first day on board and alongside in the base at HMS TERROR, I was catching up on the day's intake of signals and was aware of the general hum of some traders and customers outside the cabin, when there was a knock on the door and a Chinese gentleman stuck his head round the curtain in the doorway and started, "Good morning, Sir. How are you, Sir?"

"I'm very well, thank you," I replied, wondering where this conversation was going.

"How your dinner jacket, Sir?" he then enquired.

"Absolutely fine, thank you, and I am just a little bit busy at the moment," I countered.

HMS ACHILLES - Leander Class Frigate
Commissioned: July 1970, Sold to Chile: 1990,
Washed away by Tsunami: February 2010, Scuttled: March 2010
Length: 372ft. Beam: 43ft. Draught: 15ft.
Displacement: 2,900 tons. Complement: 260.

"Very good to hear that, Sir. Here is my card, just in case you have any ploblem with the dinner jacket."

He handed me his card and I was intrigued as to why he was so preoccupied with my dinner jacket and was not trying to sell me a new suit or something else, when he solved the problem.

"You plobably don't remember me, Sir, but I make you dinner jacket when you here in ARK LOYAL in 1963. I velly pleased jacket giving you good service."

I invited him in and we enjoyed a coffee together and talked over the changes to Hong Kong, and indeed to his business in the sixteen years that had passed.

An emergency surgical operation off Vietnam.

In March 1975, ACHILLES was dispatched to stand off the coast of Vietnam to evacuate the British Embassy staff who were vacating the Embassy as the Viet Cong took over. Unfortunately, one of the ship's company began to experience severe pain in his foreskin and day by day things were deteriorating. We did not have a doctor on board, since he had been landed to deal with a severe medical problem in Hong Kong and so we signalled the medical authorities and received very detailed instructions on the operation which was now seen to be critical, if we were to save the sailor from extreme pain and possibly worse.

The pain was being caused by an extreme contraction of the foreskin, due to massive inflammation and the instructions described the procedure to effect a circumcision. Traditionally, in a ship at sea without a doctor, the First Lieutenant steps in and reads the relevant chapter in the medical book provided. We were unlucky in that the book did not cover this particular operation and so it was a case of reading the signalled instructions and making the best of it. The First Lieutenant, John, asked me to act as his assistant for the operation and we agreed we would do the deed first thing the next morning.

We decided that we needed to rehearse the procedure and I joined John in his cabin. Laid out on his desk was a banana together with a scalpel and one prophylactic. He then explained the plan as he peeled the banana and fitted the contraceptive over one end. I was to hold the "banana" steady as he used the scalpel to make the 360-degree incision to remove the offending rubber "skin".

It was at this point that the Chief GI knocked politely and popped his head around the curtain in the cabin doorway, with the intention of asking the First Lieutenant to approve the draft of Daily Orders for the 'morrow. He took one look at the two Lieutenant Commanders, one holding a naked banana with a condom attached whilst the other appeared ready to do some damage with a scalpel. He coughed.

"I am not quite sure what's going on, Sirs," he said with a very broad grin, "but I'll pop back in five minutes."

John and I fell about laughing until we realized that this incident would be around the ship in minutes. There was little point in calling the Chief GI back and trying to explain what officers did in their cabins in their spare time, so we carried on and completed our dummy run and were both surprised at how very nervous and shaky we were, even when practicing on a banana.

It was with considerable relief when I was woken early next morning by the pipe "Hands to Flying Stations." Someone in Hong Kong had found a helicopter with sufficient fuel tanks to reach us off Vietnam and the passenger was a real doctor with the necessary skills and experience to complete the procedure that morning. The patient was relieved, in both senses of the word.

The Brazilian lacy tops

On our return from the Far East, we rounded the Cape of Good Hope and headed for Salvador in Brazil. The helicopter pilot and I stepped ashore to explore the delights of the city and soon found ourselves in a two-storey wooden shopping emporium. The ancient building had a charm of its own and contained fruit and vegetable outlets on the ground floor and tiny shops and bars on the first floor. We risked all to get up the rickety steps to the upper level and strolled around the various shops. Before long we spotted a dilapidated place selling the most exquisite lace tops, best suited to tall blonde ladies dressing for that special occasion. Since we both reckoned we had wives who fitted this category, we approached the vendor, called Felipe.

We both identified a top to our taste, but luckily not the same one, and asked the price.

"Forty ickies[11] each," he replied.

We did the conversion and thought that was about £16 and started the traditional bargaining process. After five minutes, we thought we had done quite well, getting him down to thirty-five ickies each, but when he appeared reluctant to go lower, we hung them back up and started to walk away. He pursued us and we returned. We negotiated and walked away again and this went on a few times until we said we wanted to think about it and were going to get a beer. He very quickly directed us to the best bar, some fifty feet away, just around the corner of the market on the same level.

The beer was good and we were into our second when Felipe appeared, holding both tops and the new special price of twenty-five ickies each. We thanked him, but demurred to accept the offer, saying we would have a look around and probably see him later. We downed the beers and continued shopping. The market was laid out as a square and our tour took us past Felipe's shop about half an hour later and surprise-surprise, there he was holding the tops as we

---

[11] Sailors are renowned for forgetting the name of the currency of the country they are visiting and so resort to the universal currency, the 'icky', the conversion rate for which varies considerably, depending on what you paid for something.

approached. The bartering continued for probably another five minutes and the price came down marginally, until we pleaded heat exhaustion and repaired to the same bar. Half way through the first beer, Felipe appeared again, tops in hand, and with an improved price.

Sufficient to say that the routine continued for just over two hours and very many beers, until we reached a price, for both tops, of twenty ickies. My goodness, hadn't we done well, we thought until we paid Felipe and he then embraced the bar owner, Rafael, with a huge hug and a kiss.

"You obviously know Rafael," we said to Felipe.

"Oh yes, he's my brother," said Felipe with a grin.

We settled up with Rafael and when we counted the total number of beers consumed in the last two hours, we reckoned we had spent just over one hundred and twenty ickies.

The really good news however, is that both of our wives really did think we had done rather well and wore the tops to many occasions with great style.

Collision at sea

In 1975, HMS ACHILLES was proceeding up channel past Dover and I had turned in at about 2330. I was awoken by the most almighty sound and a deceleration of the ship that caused me to slide up the bunk towards the bows of the ship, crashing my head against the wardrobe. I was awake in a flash, but concerned that there was no sign of the normal red lighting in the cabin, which I always left on in case I needed to get up in a hurry. I presumed that we had lost power, always a major concern and also worried that whatever had caused this tremendous noise and physical motion had resulted in the deck-head in my cabin collapsing on top of me and I was accordingly pinned to the bunk by something resting on my face and body. I managed to get my arms up to my face and prepared to use all my strength to force whatever was pinning me down, just enough to crawl out from underneath.

The planning board which had been ripped from the aftermost bulkhead in my cabin fell away, and feeling rather foolish and with the red light bathing the cabin, I was able to scramble into a pair of overalls and boots to investigate the crisis which was developing. At this, the main broadcast announced, "Hands to Emergency Stations," a pipe used only under extremely serious conditions. About 95% of the ship's company of two hundred and fifty were required to muster, at the rush, on the flight deck and be prepared to abandon ship if required.

My emergency station, on the other hand, was one deck immediately below my cabin in the Operations Room, together with a skeleton crew of two Ratings. It soon became clear what had happened. We had been involved in a serious collision with an oil tanker and although at that stage it was not entirely clear how extensive the damage was, sufficient to say it was potentially extremely dangerous, in that we were sitting in a vast lake of crude oil[12] on the sea around us. Moreover, we had suffered enormous damage to the bows and the first twenty feet of this frigate had collapsed and had been concertinaed into nothing and this squashed section contained the inflammable store with its cargo of highly unstable liquids.

---

[12] We found out later that the tanker had lost 10,000tons of oil.

MY BAGS ARE IN THE BACK

HMS ACHILLES in Devonport Dockyard, 1975.

25ft of the bow crushed into a few inches

While those on the bridge and in the machinery control room were checking and assessing the situation, it was decided to make our way very gently towards Portsmouth. After a while I noticed that whilst we were on a steady course, the radar display in the Ops room was slowly but surely rotating, which, in theory, at least, was not possible. I shot down two decks below to the gyro compass room and spotted the problem. The shock had caused two delicate pins at the base of the gyro to be dislodged and the gyro was merrily precessing away to its own content. Instead of heading for Portsmouth we were making for France. We corrected this and slowly but surely the gyro settled back to the correct alignment.

Shortly after that came the first example of the sailors' humour as I stuck my head out of the Ops room door on the port side to investigate a bit of a commotion. The damage control party had been instructed to shore up the collision bulkhead, the particularly strengthened bulkhead just aft of the damage, which was designed to withstand just this type of damage. As my head emerged into the passageway, two sailors appeared from behind me, at the rush, and holding a vast 10ft long, 6 x 6 inch wooden shore. Just before it decapitated me, the nearest sailor started imitating a fire engine with a very realistic "dee-dah-dee-dah" followed by, "Nearly got you Sir."

Meanwhile on the flight deck, I was to be told later, the conditions were not at all good. It was foggy and therefore very cold and many of the ship's company were not appropriately clothed, but this did not apparently dampen spirits. One young sailor approached one of the officers with: "Thought we might have a bit of quiz, Sir, to keep spirits up. What's grey, begins with 'A' and f…s tankers?"

It was about two hours later when I decided in the Ops room that one of the two lads could be spared to take a few minutes to brew up a cup of tea.

"Great idea," said the other one, " but do you think you could, um, er, 'adjust your dress' so to speak, Sir?"

It transpired that in the rush to get up, I had failed to dress correctly and my best friend had been, shall we say, threatening to knock things off the chart table for the last two hours and the two sailors had not seen fit to tell me. That at least is what I like to think, although they assured me later that they hadn't noticed it until then. Damned cheek.

The tanker concerned was the Greek tanker Olympic Alliance and the damage caused to both ships was extensive and expensive. The crude oil lost was 10,000 tons of Iranian light crude and although I cannot recall the total cost, I believe that when the Greek company brought a case against the RN in 1984/85, they were seeking something in excess of £10 million.

Immediately after the collision I instructed my deputy to ensure that all possible performance figures for the two radar sets which might bear upon any subsequent investigation should be recorded, witnessed and signed by the senior maintainer.

I kept these records for ten years until the case was held in London, at which time I was serving in Whitehall as a Commander working for the Naval Secretary. One day I answered a telephone call from the Admiral's secretary, coincidentally my cousin Jonathan, by now a barrister and soon to be Chief Naval Judge Advocate for the Navy, who told me I had been summoned by the court to answer charges that the radars had not been operating correctly at the time of the incident, ten years previously and I was to present myself as soon as convenient that day.

"Could you let the court know that I need to collect the record of the maintenance state and performance figures from my flat and that I would be able to attend the court at 1400 if that was convenient to the court," I told Jonathan.

As I packed up my office to leave for my flat, Jonathan rang again and said, "I told the court you were on your way and the Greek company have settled out of court."

Supermarket trollies in Cowes

Cowes week on the Isle of Wight traditionally demanded the presence of a warship as a guardship and it was our turn in 1976. It was also a tradition that the guardship would offer assistance to the harbourmaster, by providing divers to help with any underwater problems such as moorings which had been disturbed or damaged during the busy week, or even competitors who had managed to drop something valuable overboard. At that time, I was also the diving officer and in the first two days we carried out a couple of small jobs for the harbourmaster as well as recovering a very expensive pair of binoculars for a German skipper.

On the third day, the harbourmaster had no need for divers apart from a general scavenge around the marina to identify and remove any possible hazards. I spent half an hour or so swimming under the pontoons without finding anything important and returned to the surface to supervise the next two divers. We moved across the marina and within ten minutes the divers surfaced, dragging a supermarket trolley with them. Surprisingly it even contained some tins, a bottle of milk and packets of food, all of which were in exceptionally good condition. The trolley was also sparkling clean and we agreed that the supermarket would probably enjoy being re-united with their property. The two Able Seamen who had found the trolley offered to return it to the supermarket.

"All very well lads," said I, "but how do we know which supermarket?"

I immediately regretted the question as they replied, "For goodness sake Sir. The price stickers are still on the food."

"Off you go then; we'll stay here."

Ten minutes later, they came back grinning from ear to ear and waving two ten-pound notes. The manager had been delighted and thought their efforts deserved such recognition. We agreed that the team would share the reward and that lunchtime we had a beer to celebrate.

The next day we did a couple of jobs and with no other need for our services, I suggested we should return to the ship, anchored off Cowes.

"I think we should check the rest of the marina," chipped in one of the divers who had found the trolley.

"It's highly unlikely we'll find another," I replied. "And don't forget we covered most of the marina yesterday."

"Still worth a quick look," persisted the Able Seaman. "I think we should look over there," he added, pointing to a particular pontoon.

At this I thought, 'Oh no, they didn't go and push one in last night, did they?'

A few minutes later and they were in the water and within ten minutes, they surfaced dragging, guess what? – a trolley. I could not condone them taking this back to the supermarket and seeking a further reward and told them so.

"Don't worry, Sir, it's a different supermarket from yesterday," they grinned.

They really had thought it through. I said I wanted absolutely nothing to do with it, but if they wanted to buy the diving team a beer, then who was I to argue, and that is what we did.

A brief visit to Rockall

Anyone who has listened to the shipping forecast has heard of Rockall but not too many people have visited this very small island, lying approximately 186 miles west of St Kilda, which is 41 miles west of Benbecula in the Outer Hebrides, and 267 miles from the nearest point on the Irish mainland. In other words, it is a long way from anywhere. It is not so much an island as an outcrop or even perhaps better described as a rock. It measures about 82ft on its north-south axis and 72ft on its east-west axis and the summit is 56 feet above mean sea level.

The island, or rock, is the core of an eroded volcano that erupted around 55 million years ago. On 18th September 1955 at 1016 GMT, Britain claimed Rockall, apparently to stop the Russians spying on Corporal missile tests. The islet was within reach of a planned guided missile range on South Uist, Outer Hebrides and the British government feared foreign spies could use it as an observation post.

A group was landed comprising two Royal Marines and a civilian naturalist, led by Royal Navy officer Lieutenant Commander Desmond Scott. They were deposited on the island by a Royal Navy helicopter from HMS Vidal. Having raised a Union flag on the island, they cemented a plaque into the rock.

Rockall
"The most isolated speck of rock, surrounded by water, on the surface of the Earth."
J.A.Macintosh (1946)
"There can be no place more desolate, despairing and awful."
Lord Kennet (1971)

The inscription on the plaque read:

"By authority of Her Majesty Queen Elizabeth the Second, by the Grace of God of the United Kingdom of Great Britain and Northern Ireland and of her other realms and territories, Queen, Head of the Commonwealth, Defender of the Faith, etc, etc, etc. And in accordance with Her Majesty's instructions dated the 14.9.55, a landing was effected this day upon this island of Rockall from H.M.S. Vidal. The Union flag was hoisted and possession of the island was taken in the name of Her Majesty.

[Signed] R H Connell, Captain, H.M.S. Vidal, 18 September 1955."

In 1972, the Isle of Rockall Act was passed, which made Rockall officially part of the District of Harris, Inverness-shire, Scotland. This represented the last territorial expansion of the British Empire.

In 1975/76 HMS ACHILLES was deployed to land a British National on the rock as a show of strength and commitment that it was British territory. The day was rough with an enormous swell and strong gusts of wind. Clearly it would have to be a helicopter landing and it was soon decided that the best choice for a landing would be someone who could swim back to the ship, should things go awry, a ship's diver. I got my dry-suit on and joined the First Lieutenant who, as a Fleet Air Arm Observer, had volunteered to act as the winchman. The pilot took us so close that I was actually able to step onto the very top of the rock and attach myself immediately to the beacon atop the rock, which as I remember, was three feet in diameter, and took up most of the standing room on the summit. The ledge around the beacon was only, roughly, one foot wide.

The downwash from the helicopter was considerable as the First Lieutenant passed me the various bits of equipment I needed. This comprised a ship's crest, a bucket of cement with a trowel, a bottle of champagne in a sealed plastic tube that also contained a copy of ACHILLES's Daily Orders and finally a lump hammer and chisel. The crest and the champagne were duly secured for the next visitor to examine and sample and I set about my paleontological challenge. The Instructor Officer on board was extremely keen to have a sample of the rock and I had said that this should be simple enough.

At this stage, the helicopter was in the hover a few yards away and the Observer and the Pilot were watching as I tried to secure the bucket, hold the hammer and chisel and still remain firmly attached to the beacon while trying to chisel a small sample from the rock. It was soon clear that we needed to get the bucket back to the helicopter and they approached and I was able to pass it across. The pilot then decided he preferred the view where he was, extremely close to the rock, and the Observer pointed to his watch and indicated that he thought I should get a move on.

It was not simply a matter of kneeling down to use the chisel. The beacon and the lack of space on the ledge made this extremely tricky. With the helicopter down-wash complicating matters, I bent down and started to chip away. When I felt that the sample was about to give way to my hammering and decided to give it one more gentle tap, I placed the chisel at the appropriate point and was about to strike, when the sample decided to part company with the rock. It sprang away and as I tried to grasp it, it flew gracefully away and bounced down the side of the rock and inevitably into the sea.

Unfortunately for me, the pilot had been watching this and found this so hilarious that, as a reflex, he doubled up laughing. This, understandably, caused him to lean on the cyclic and the helicopter responded. As the helicopter dipped towards the waves below, I was working out how I was going to jump far enough away from the rock, to clear it, as I jumped into the sea to rescue the pilot and Observer, when the engine noise surged and then my colleagues reappeared, still grinning like Cheshire cats. The Instructor Officer did get his sample and so too did the three of us involved in the claim on this British outcrop.

Since 1997, the UK has only claimed a 12 nautical mile territorial sea around Rockall, acknowledging that it is legally a "rock" under Article 121 of the United Nations Convention on the Law of the Sea (UNCLOS).

Diving in Tromso harbour

Later, ACHILLES visited Tromso, north of the Arctic Circle, and steaming through the fjords as we approached was an experience in itself, especially passing so close to the spot where the TIRPITZ was sunk by the RAF. The final attack took place on November 12, 1944 when thirty Lancasters from No. 9 Squadron attacked with 12,000-pound (5,400 kg) "Tallboy" bombs. The first bombs narrowly missed the target, but then a great yellow flash burst on the foredeck and the Tirpitz was seen to tremble as it was hit by at least two Tallboys. A column of steam and smoke shot up to about 300 feet and within a few minutes the ship had started to list badly. It then suffered a tremendous explosion as the ammunition store's magazine went up. She rolled over to port and capsized. About ten minutes after the first bomb struck, the Tirpitz had completely turned turtle with only the hull visible from the air. Approximately 1000 of her crew were killed. None of the attacking aircraft were significantly damaged and all returned safely to base.

Although not flying on the raid, my uncle and godfather, Flight Lieutenant, later Squadron Leader, Peter Langdon DFM, who had already completed a full tour of 30 operations with 207 Squadron was, at the time, an instructor with 9 Squadron and became the operations officer for the Commanding Officer in this successful attack. Later, he secured a return to operations in the last few months of the war, with 9 Squadron, taking part in raids on Bremen and Lutzendorf.

Whilst alongside in the harbour, a member of the communications department managed to drop an extremely expensive naval radio set over the side and the diving team was tasked to recover it. As the diving officer, I mustered the team and briefed them, which didn't take long, comprising a brief description of the radio set and the exact point where it had been dropped. It would clearly have dropped like a stone, there was no current and the visibility in the icy water was practically unlimited, a luxury that we were not used to in Portsmouth harbour.

Expecting the search to last no more than a few moments, I was surprised when the two divers returned to the surface, indicated the normal thumbs up that they were fine and then exchanged a few words with the poor communicator, sitting in the diving boat, who, by now was looking increasingly worried about the cost of the set, which some of the team were suggesting was in the region of a thousand pounds. Down they went again, but after another ten minutes, returned with the same shake of the head, indicating a lack of success. Another, rather longer conversation took place with the communicator and when I saw one of the divers shake his hand, I was unable to control my curiosity and leant forward to catch the last part of the conversation, which seemed to suggest that a certain beer ration was going to change hands for the next few weeks.

At this point I intervened and handing over responsibility for the dive to the other trained supervisor, entered the water to join the two devious divers. Needless to say, the radio was immediately beneath the diving boat and clearly visible, almost from the surface. We returned the radio to the communicator and I'm glad to say that thirty-six hours later, following a good fresh water wash and drying session, it was perfectly serviceable.

Meanwhile we had a diving team in the water, in extremely cold conditions, which provided us with a good opportunity to experience the conditions and inspect the underside of the ship and the many openings in the hull for the various seawater services. We swam the 370ft length of the ship on both sides and finding nothing untoward, I indicated to the other two that we would move towards the edge of an obvious ledge beneath the ship, which extended about twenty metres from the harbour wall. The depth of the water was probably no more than twenty-five feet and as we approached the edge of the ledge, we could see that the water past the edge of the ledge was getting noticeably darker as the water depth increased.

The drop, when we got to the edge was almost vertical, but what was even more dramatic was the sight beneath us. All three of us lay there motionless, hovering over a German cruiser, lying on her side, some thirty metres beneath us. The water was so clear that one could see her from stem to stern in the most ghostly but grey detail. It was clearly an eerie sight and yet almost beautiful in the extreme sense of the word but of course it brought to mind that it was certainly a war-grave and due the respect that it demanded.

Postscript. Looking back, I find it difficult to believe that I didn't research the history of the ship at that time and to this day, some forty years later, I have failed to determine her name or the circumstances surrounding her sinking.

How not to talk to your Captain

We were at sea in the Western Approaches and supposed to be conducting an exercise with a submarine but matters were conspiring against us. The weather was really foul with a massive sea, making it extremely difficult to make one's way around the ship and also making it virtually impossible to detect a submarine using our hull-mounted sonar. The final straw came when the sonar maintainer reported that the set had suffered a major problem in the main power supply cabinet and furthermore he was suffering from a severe bout of seasickness.

The sonar instrument space was for'd and subject to the worst of ship movement when pitching in a heavy sea and the maintainer had been there for well over an hour, nursing the set to maintain optimum performance. When the Chief Artificer and I arrived to establish the scale of the problem, matters got even worse as the maintainer opened a large High Voltage power supply drawer and promptly attempted to fill it with what can only be politely described as a "Technicolor yawn".

We sent the maintainer away to recover and the Chief and I set about clearing up the mess and more importantly trying to restore power to the sonar so that we could at least appear to be trying to detect the submarine. At this point the internal communication line from the Operations Room sounded and I found myself talking to a very agitated Principal Warfare Officer (PWO). This young Lieutenant had, I recall, a particularly high-pitched voice, especially when he got exasperated.

"The Captain wants to know precisely what's going on and how long before he can have his sonar system back on line."

I replied that we had major problems with the power supply to the set and that this had been made worse by the ingress of some 'water' into the cabinet. I considered that it would be a minimum of 15 minutes before we could even identify the cause of the failure, but I would keep the PWO informed of any progress. I found his response of, "Make sure you do," unhelpful and downright insolent when talking to a senior officer. I made a note to talk to him later about his attitude.

Three minutes later and the telephone buzzed again.

"How's it going WEO? The Captain is getting really upset," he whined.

Again I explained that it was early days and that I had nothing to report since our chat three minutes ago and that conditions up for'd were extremely unpleasant and, at times, downright dangerous as we bounced around the instrument space and tried to measure very high voltage levels. I also pointed out that every minute I spent talking to him was a minute wasted in resolving the problem, but if he wanted to come down and lend a hand, he would be most welcome. He demurred and ended with another unnecessary, "Keep me informed."

By this time the Chief and I decided to remove the 'sickened' power drawer and replace it with a spare unit from the other side of the instrument space. Alongside in harbour this would take a matter of a few minutes, but the ship motion turned this into a major evolution. As we slid the defective drawer from the cabinet and were assailed by the ghastly and sickening odour, the telephone buzzed yet again. The level of squeakiness in the PWO's voice had now risen to soprano-like levels.

"The Captain wants to see you on the bridge, NOW."

I remonstrated that this would ensure a further delay but the PWO then astounded me by saying that he had told the Captain that he, the PWO, did not think we were making sufficient progress or devoting enough effort to solving the problem and that he considered that the time had come for the WEO to have an "interview without coffee" with the Captain on the bridge.

I was more than angry and slammed the telephone down. I briefed the Chief to carry on and see what he could achieve and I would return as soon as I could. I set off to navigate the one hundred feet of passageways and the four ladders up to the bridge, with the ship rolling and pitching as before. When I arrived on the darkened bridge, it may have been the sight of the Captain, safely secure in his special chair with spring-loaded suspension, while I staggered across the bridge and bounced off the pelorus before managing to hang on to the edge of the signalman's desk, which caused me to lose all sense of propriety and respect.

"Ah, there you are WEO. What's the problem with the sonar

then?" he enquired, taking another sip of tea.

"Do you want the technical or the layman's explanation?" I replied.

"The technical one of course, WEO."

"It's totally f...d, Sir."

"I don't think there's any need for that attitude WEO," he replied and went on to say he would see me later when I had calmed down.

We did eventually get the sonar on line; we did complete the exercise with the submarine and much later I did have a conversation with the Captain, which ended with both of us agreeing that things could have been handled better. The PWO however did not leave my cabin feeling so pleased with the outcome of the very one-sided conversation in which he was not invited to take part.

1978/79 - HMS CENTURION

The Functional Costing System – Three years into two

I was then appointed to HMS Centurion, the Pay and Drafting authority in Gosport as a Systems Analyst in the Computer department. When I joined, I had no idea what was ahead of me until I was summoned to London to meet an Admiral, the Director General of Naval Manpower and Training, in Whitehall. He explained that he wanted me to design and produce a system that would provide the Naval Staff with detailed costs for running each and every ship and naval establishment over the next ten years. The system was required to reflect the rank or rating of every man or woman involved throughout the service, their basic pay and the various allowances or special services pay, that they might be entitled to, as well as the state of operational deployment or repair for each unit of the fleet.

The Admiral tasked me to go away and consider whether this could be achieved within three years and I returned to Gosport to discuss the requirement with my computer systems experts. We decided that it was indeed possible to achieve the desired output and that we could do it within two and not three years. The Admiral was obviously pleased and we set to.

The system we designed and built became known as the Functional Costing System. It was to be run once each year on the largest computer mainframe in the RN, to provide the Naval Staff with the necessary planning tool, providing them with an enquiry-answering tool as well as providing them with the necessary input to the Naval component of the Defence Estimates. The program was so

MY BAGS ARE IN THE BACK

large and complex that it consumed every hard drive and the entire processing power available in the establishment and could only run overnight. Some purists argued that we could and indeed should have designed a more efficient system that would not have used so many hard drives and tied up the central processor for such a long time. I felt and still feel, that they failed to understand the beauty of the design, which enabled amendments to be incorporated very quickly and simply and most importantly to be incorporated by those who would maintain the system in the years ahead when those involved in the initial construction, had moved on.

It was completed within the two year timeframe and proved to be an 'excellent' planning tool, according to those higher up the food chain.

1979 - ADMIRALTY UNDERWATER WEAPONS ESTABLISHMENT (AUWE)

Memories of the spy story of 1961 – the year I joined the Navy

Just over eighteen years before I joined AUWE, and in the same year that I had joined the Royal Navy in 1961, the establishment was the centre of what became known as the Portland Spy Ring, a spy ring that operated in England from the late 1950s until 1961 when the core of the network was arrested by the British security services. It is one of the most famous examples of the use of illegal residents - spies who operate in a foreign country but without the cover of their embassy. Its members included Harry Houghton, Ethel Gee, Gordon Lonsdale and Morris and Lona Cohen (a.k.a. Peter and Helen Kroger).

The Portland Spy Ring was so significant in the 60s and of such importance to the RN's submarine service, that the basic facts are repeated here.

In 1959 the CIA received letters from a mole, codenamed Sniper (who later turned out to be Michael Goleniewski). Sniper said information was reaching the Russians from the Admiralty Underwater Weapons Establishment and HMS Osprey at Portland, England, where the Royal Navy tested equipment for undersea warfare.

Suspicion fell on Harry Houghton, a former sailor who was a civil service clerk at the base. MI5 put Houghton under surveillance. They also watched his mistress, Ethel Gee. She was a filing clerk who

MY BAGS ARE IN THE BACK

handled documents that Houghton himself did not have access to. They often went to London, where they would meet a man identified as Gordon Lonsdale, a Canadian businessman. During these meetings Lonsdale and Houghton exchanged packages.

MI5 promptly put Lonsdale under surveillance. It was found that Lonsdale often went to 45 Cranley Drive, Ruislip in Middlesex to visit an antiquarian bookseller at home, Peter Kroger and his wife Helen. The Krogers were also put under close but discreet watch.

On Saturday 7 January 1961, Houghton, Gee and Lonsdale were meeting in London when they were arrested by Special Branch Detective Superintendent George Gordon Smith. Gee's shopping bag contained huge amounts of film and photographs of classified material, including details of HMS Dreadnought, Britain's first nuclear submarine, and the stalling speed specifications of the Borg Warner torque converter.

Smith and two colleagues then went to Ruislip to see the Krogers. Claiming to be investigating some local burglaries they gained entry to the house. Once inside they identified themselves as Special Branch officers and said that the Krogers had to accompany them to Scotland Yard for questioning. Before leaving, Mrs Kroger asked to be allowed to stoke up the boiler. Before she could, Smith insisted on checking her handbag first. It was found to contain microdots, the photographic reduction of documents in order to make them small enough to be smuggled more easily. Smith, a veteran spy catcher, had guessed her intention to destroy these microdots.

The microdots found at the Krogers' home were letters sent between Lonsdale and his wife, who lived in the USSR with their children. These included things like money matters and how the children were doing at school. Kroger had used the print in his antique books to hold the microdots and smuggle them between Britain and Russia. These would have included the secrets passed on by Houghton and Gee.

The Kroger house was full of spying equipment, including large sums of money, photographic material, code pads for coding messages and a long-range radio transmitter-receiver for communicating with Moscow. It took several days to unearth all the equipment, and other items including fake passports were not found until after the police had left. The MI5 intelligence stated that the

Krogers' radio transmitter was only located after nine days of searching. Over the years, during subsequent renovations, several other radio transmitters were unearthed. Large amounts of money were also found in the homes of Houghton, Gee and Lonsdale.

Two days after their arrest, all five were charged with espionage at Bow Street Magistrates Court. Gee and the Krogers protested their innocence; Houghton tried to turn Queen's Evidence but was refused; Lonsdale maintained complete silence. The trial began on Monday 13 March 1961.

In giving evidence, Gee claimed that as far as she knew, Lonsdale was Alex Johnson, an American naval Commander who wanted to know how the British were handling information passed on by the United States. She had had no idea that the information was actually going to the Russians. She had gone along out of love for Houghton, her first lover after a lifetime of spinsterhood. Houghton claimed that he had been the subject of threats by mystery men and beatings by thugs if he failed to pass on information. These men had also made threats concerning Gee and Houghton's ex-wife. He too, he claimed, had only known Lonsdale as Alex Johnson and he tried desperately to minimise Gee's involvement.

Neither Lonsdale nor the Krogers took the stand, but in statements read out in court, Lonsdale took responsibility. He claimed that the Krogers were innocent: he had often looked after their house while they were away and had used it to hide his spying equipment without their knowledge. Peter and Helen Kroger backed up this claim, saying that Peter was simply an antiquarian bookseller and Helen a housewife. But they could not explain why fake Canadian passports with their photos were found in the house, and clearly intended for a possible get-away.

The jury returned verdicts of guilty for all of the accused. The Special Branch Detective Superintendent then took the stand. He announced that through their fingerprints, the Krogers had been identified as Morris and Lona Cohen, renowned spies who had worked with Ethel and Julius Rosenberg, Rudolf Abel and David Greenglass in the United States. Smith also revealed Cohen's past life in the military and scholastic service.

On the other hand, Lonsdale remained a man of mystery in spite of extensive inquiries by MI5, the FBI, the Royal Canadian Mounted

Police and other Western intelligence services. They were convinced that he was an actual Russian and a member of the KGB, but so far his past could only be traced back as far as 1954 when he had first appeared in Canada.

Houghton and Gee were sentenced to 15 years in prison. They were released in 1970 and married the following year.

The Krogers (i.e. the Cohens) were sentenced to 20 years' jail. In 1969, they were exchanged for the British citizen Gerald Brooke, who had been arrested by the Russians. As part of the process, the Soviets confirmed that they were spies.

Lonsdale, the mastermind, was sentenced to 25 years. In 1964 he was exchanged for the British spy Greville Wynne, who had been arrested in Russia. His real name was revealed to be Konon Trofimovich Molody.

It is believed that the ring numbered more than the five who were arrested, but these would have included staff at the Russian and Polish embassies, who would have been immune from prosecution anyway.

*

Even though eighteen years had passed since the discovery of the spy ring at Portland, I felt that the establishment still retained a definite aura of importance and security awareness as I entered its portals on the first day of May 1979, especially since I knew that my appointment was specifically directed towards the technical aspects of submarines which had involved Houghton, Lonsdale and the Krugers, those eighteen years ago.

Submarines are designed to operate silently beneath the waves and the navy was building an improved acoustic range off the Scottish coast where a submarine's acoustic signature could be measured and recorded and any anomalies identified and rectified. My appointment, as the Deputy Project Manager for this range, the British Underwater Test and Evaluation Centre (BUTEC), involved the development of the support facilities and the technical areas of the range. After six months in this extremely interesting, and highly classified, appointment, I was selected for promotion to Commander and moved on to a new post in London.

1980/1981 - MOD, DIRECTORATE NAVAL MANAGEMENT SYSTEMS, DATA PROCESSING POLICY

On promotion to Commander, I was appointed to the Ministry of Defence and this time to Northumberland House[13] in Northumberland Avenue, just off Trafalgar Square. The architecture of the building certainly reflected its history as a grand hotel, with an amazing entrance and adjacent ballroom decorated with an abundance of pink marble. In its day, the hotel was purported to be a place of assignation for the Prince of Wales and Lillie Langtree. Their affair was said to be torrid and long lasting. The Prince once complained to Langtry, "I've spent enough on you to build a battleship," whereupon she tartly replied, "And you've spent enough in me to float one."

When I arrived on my first day, I was pointed in the direction of my new office on the fourth floor and was delighted to find I didn't have to share. The office was certainly small, but it was fitted out with the usual furniture and filing cabinets. Reflecting on the office I had just left in Portland where I had a one hundred and eighty degree

---

[13] Originally completed in 1887, The Northumberland, Northumberland Avenue, was built as the 500-room 'Grand Hotel'.

view of the English Channel, I wandered over to the window to admire the view over London. The telephone exchange opposite the window was approximately six feet away and the building extended as far as the eye could see in both dimensions, up/down and left/right. On opening the window, the Portland memories of seagulls and fresh air were replaced by the incessant twittering of the telephone exchange and the unmistakable smell of city traffic.

The Garden Party at Buckingham Palace

During this appointment, I was lucky enough to be allocated two of the Ministry of Defence tickets for the annual garden party at Buckingham Palace and my wife immediately sought a new outfit, whereas I found my clothes brush and gave the uniform a quick brush down. On the day of the event, my wife arrived at my office in good time and at the appropriate moment, we made our way down to Northumberland Avenue, where taxis abounded, day and night. My wife asked me whether I would mind if she summoned the taxi and told him our destination, on the basis that this was something she had always wanted to do.

As the summoned taxi drew in, the taxi driver leant across and looked my wife in the eye.

"Bleedin' Bucking'm Palace for you then, is it?"

A breakdown in Parliament Square

I had a flat in Ebury Street during the appointment and cycled the two miles into work most days. One summer evening I had been attending a meeting in the MOD Main Building and set off for the flat down Whitehall. The traffic lights at Parliament Square were red and I found myself on the front row of the grid, and since I was intending to go up Victoria Street, I was in the third of the four lanes, which was the centre one of the three 'ahead' lanes. The traffic built up behind me, but this posed no threat as long as one got away promptly and got to the slow lane of the three lanes turning right into Victoria Street, in good time.

As the lights turned amber and green, I was away. Well, strictly speaking, I was normally 'away', but on this particular day, absolutely nothing happened. As I stood on the right-hand pedal, the bike felt as though it had been standing in quick-setting concrete for an hour. The bike moved not a single centimetre. So there I was, standing amidst four lanes of traffic that, as ever, was intent on getting through the square like lightning. As they sped past, inches either side of me, there was nothing to be done except wait for the next red light, which seemed to take hours instead of the usual couple of minutes.

When I eventually reached the pavement and inspected the problem, expecting to find something jamming the pedal, the chain or even the wheel itself, I could see that the rear wheel was out of line and very firmly touching the frame. Presuming that one of the axle-nuts was loose, I checked them both and was surprised to find them secure. However, I still considered that they were the cause of the wheel slewing to one side and so proceeded to slacken them off, realign the wheel and re-tighten them. Feeling confident that my engineering skills had been put to good use, I decided to test the bike before taking on Parliament Square and felt rather foolish when the bike failed to move again, as soon as I tried to cycle away from the kerb.

I re-inspected the wheel and the axle-nuts and then realised that the whole wheel was actually moving laterally even when the nuts were fully tightened. It was time to remove the whole wheel and inspect the problem more carefully. Having slackened the nuts and slipped the chain clear of the derailleur gear system, I heard a metallic clink as I eased the wheel away from the frame. Looking down, I was amazed to see an oily, two-inch stud, with a washer and nut attached, lying on the pavement and was wondering where that had come from, when I suddenly realised that the nut looked suspiciously like the axle-nut itself.

When I turned the wheel round, I saw that the left-hand axle-nut was missing, and that the wheel hub was empty, by which I mean I could see the ball bearings and there was no sign of the axle itself. At this stage, it was clear, and perhaps it should have been clear much sooner, that the axle had broken.

Two days later, the replacement axle took only minutes to fit and I was able to return to the streets of London, but I admit that thenceforth, I approached Parliament Square with respect and some trepidation.

1982-1983 - HMS GLAMORGAN

HMS GLAMORGAN - County Class Destroyer
Commissioned: October 1966, Sold to Chile: 1986.
Sunk at sea on the way to the breakers: 2005.
Length: 520ft. Beam: 53ft. Draught: 20ft.
Displacement: 6,200 tons. Complement: 500.

I joined HMS GLAMORGAN on the 1st March 1982 and a month later we were off Gibraltar conducting missile test firings, together with other destroyers. The Commander-in-Chief Fleet, Admiral Sir John Fieldhouse was on board and had taken up residence in the Admiral's accommodation forward. One evening, the officers decided to watch a film in the wardroom and at a particularly tense moment in the film, a door from the wardroom into the Captain's day-cabin was opened and bright lighting flooded the screen.

"Shut that b....y door," grumbled someone from the rear of the stalls.

"So sorry," came a timid and squeaky reply, "but do you have a copy of Jane's Fighting Ships?"

We then realised that 'Squeaky' was the Admiral's Flag Lieutenant and we had better oblige. The film was stopped and on went the main lights. The book was quickly located in the wardroom library and we sent him on his way, mumbling his apologies and thanks. Ten minutes, the film had progressed to the point where the hero was, or at least we all hoped he was, about to make an advance towards the very pretty heroine, when the same door opened and light flooded the screen again.

"Oh really! For goodness sake! Now what?" came the same voice from the back.

"Do you happen to have a copy of Jane's Fighting Aircraft?" came Squeaky's next request.

This too was handed over and we returned to the film. However, we were not to enjoy the possible moment of passion on screen, since a few moments we heard the pipe, "Hands to Flying Stations" . Since it was now about 2130 and there had been no plans for night flying on the programme, we realised that something significant was up. It was the night of 1st/2nd April and the Argentinians were on the move and invading the Falkland Islands. Admiral Fieldhouse was airlifted to Gibraltar and onwards home to UK to take overall Command of Operations.

We headed south and it was to be another 104 days before we were to put a foot ashore again.

Exocet concerns

A lot has been written about the conflict and this is not the place to repeat the details of our involvement, but it is the place to remember the fourteen shipmates who died as a result of the Exocet attack on the ship on 12th June. We will remember them.

GLAMORGAN had four Exocet missiles, fitted in their sealed canisters, just aft of the turret on the fo'c'sle and we fully understood the characteristics and limitations of the system. The Exocet threat was real as we headed south, and we knew which Argentinian ships and aircraft were Exocet-capable and we were in no doubt that they would deploy and use the missiles. One small part of defending oneself was to use chaff and place it relative to the ship such that the incoming missile would be seduced to attack the silver paper target generated by the chaff, fly through it and eventually run out of power and ditch harmlessly in the sea. The missiles, in those days, had a range of twenty miles and they were launched in the general direction of a target and would then activate the inbuilt radar system at a point ten miles from the expected position of the target. The radar in the missile would then search from near to far and from left to right and would acquire and lock onto the first target it located. The missiles would fly at one of three pre-determined heights above the sea; this height being set by the launching vehicle and could not be changed once launched.

Clearly, the best place to position the chaff cloud was ahead of the ship and on the starboard bow. However, if your ship was steaming, at 28 knots, to attack a surface ship, such as the ARA General Belgrano[14], and there was a headwind of say, 25 knots, then the chaff would be moving aft at 53 knots (61 mph) and would be useless as a means of distraction after just a few moments. We needed to know how often to fire a new chaff distraction cloud ahead of the ship. I designed a plastic calculator with inputs of wind speed and relative direction and ship's speed, which produced the requisite firing rate.

We soon realised that we would run out of chaff, if we were to face many such challenges and we needed a better solution. This is where

---

[14] A task which we were later tasked to do in conjunction with two frigates.

the idea of deploying our Wessex helicopter arose and we fabricated a large metal radar reflector in the classic diamond-shape and suspended it from the airframe. The pilot flew to the appropriate spot ahead of the ship, on the starboard bow, and yes, we did remember to remind him of the three heights at which the Exocet could fly and suggested he flew slightly higher than the greatest of the three.

There was one other major concern I had and that was the matter of where an incoming Exocet might hit the ship. GLAMORGAN had a magazine full of Seaslug missiles, laid flat, and the magazine ran two-thirds the length of the ship on number two deck. These two-ton missiles, twenty feet in length had one serious drawback in that the four wrap-round boost missiles were extremely sensitive to physical shock and shrapnel from a missile strike would almost certainly cause ignition. If one booster was ignited, the consequences were probably going to be disastrous for the ship as there would be sympathetic ignitions from nearby boosters and although the magazine was divided by flash doors and the missile immediately behind was protected by a deflecting plate, no one was entirely certain if we would survive.

Having studied the height above the sea at which Exocet would fly in its terminal phase, I realised we did have two very strong parts of the ship, namely the bow and the stern, which would absorb a lot of the energy and more importantly waste a few precious milliseconds as the missile impacted. The Exocet has a fuse delay of 14 milliseconds from impact to detonation, to allow the missile to penetrate the ship's skin and of course, cause more damage by containing the power of the explosion within the confines of the ship. If we could take the impact on the bows, then the enormous weight and bulk of the two anchors and the anchor cables in the cable locker would absorb a lot of the energy and take up the 14 milliseconds so that most of the energy of the warhead was expended into fresh air. Similarly, at the stern, we had the massive steel structure on the quarterdeck of the Seaslug launcher and behind that two thick blast doors angled at 45 degrees, which again would do the trick.

After many hours discussing the options, the Captain instructed all officers of the watch and warfare officers in the operations room, that if we were ever to detect an inbound Exocet missile we must turn either towards or away, depending on the relative angle of approach. On 12th June when we were tragically hit, it was the reaction of the watch-keeping team on the bridge that saved the day, as they saw the incoming missile just abaft the port beam and turned away at 28 knots. The turn to starboard, at that speed caused the ship to roll quite substantially and the spurn-water on the deck-edge on the portside, where the missile hit, was several feet closer to the sea and to the missile height than normal. If the missile had struck us when we were steaming normally, I am certain it would have penetrated the ship and caused catastrophic damage.

The first day at war

On 1st May, just after the Vulcan bombing raid on the Port Stanley airfield, we detached with the frigates HMS ARROW and HMS ALACRITY to bombard the airport at Port Stanley and during the process we were attacked by four Argentinian Mirage aircraft. We were operating close inshore at the time and two aircraft appeared from around a bluff and were upon us before we could react. The pilot of the attacking aircraft appeared to make a simple mistake in his bombing run by flicking his wings, as he approached from dead astern, to make both of the two 500lb bombs he was going to drop, strike the ship. He over-corrected and the two bombs, criss-crossed the ship and exploded beneath the stern, displacing an enormous amount of water, making the ship temporarily unstable.

In the Operations Room, as the ship started to roll dramatically, I heard a high pitched and young voice from somewhere in the darkness say, "We're going over," followed immediately by a deeper and more mature response, "No we're not laddie. Just get on with your plotting job. There's a good lad."

Meanwhile, damage control parties throughout the ship were searching for signs of damage inflicted by the bombs, particularly towards the stern. One matter of real concern was the welfare of the young Mechanical Engineering Rating closed up, on his own, in the cold, damp and lonely steering gear compartment, right aft beneath the water line, the 'Tiller Flat'. His task, should damage be caused to the steering gear, was to switch the system to emergency steering control. The Senior Engineer in the Machinery Control Room amidships was obviously concerned that the Rating was unhurt after what must have been a shattering effect, with two 500lb bombs exploding very close to the stern and he also wished to check the state of the steering gear itself. He telephoned the Tiller Flat.

"Are you alright down there?" he asked.

MY BAGS ARE IN THE BACK

May 1982 - Typical Falklands sea conditions ... a colour photograph!

After a short pause, he received a reassuring response from the young lad and was told that the equipment was functioning perfectly and there appeared to be no real damage apart from a few shattered light bulbs. He continued: "Is there anything you need then?'

"A new pair of overalls would come in handy, Sir," came the reply.

The Pebble Island raid

On 14th May we were detached in support of the SAS raid on the Argentinian Pucara aircraft on Pebble Island. However, a major problem arose as we prepared for the raid. The type 978, navigation radar, was suddenly put out of action by a burnt out motor. This motor, high on the foremast, drove the rotation of the aerial and it soon became clear that not only did we not have a spare but that no other ship in the Falklands area had a replacement motor. We needed this to be available within twelve hours. I assembled our experts and explained that we needed a solution within an hour or two and reminded them of the possibly apocryphal stories that I had heard about robbing motors from the ship's washing machines in the laundry to remedy just such a problem. "Back here in an hour with your best ideas then," I said.

When we re-assembled they came up with all sorts of ideas, most of which were impractical or too time-consuming, but there was one that caught my imagination. This involved the attachment of ropes, via pulleys, to both ends of the aerial and a couple of lads pulling on the ropes alternately to waggle the aerial back and forwards. It was not an entirely stupid idea because electromagnetic waves travel at 180,000 miles per second and the aerial would not care how fast or slow it was rotating, as long as it was pointing in the right direction occasionally, to assist the officers on the bridge and in the operations room, in navigating the ship.

I adopted this idea and suggested that instead of ropes, we should attach wind vanes to both ends of the aerial to act as a horizontal windmill. As long as the wind over the deck was five or ten knots, I assured the Captain, the aerial would rotate and he could operate the system in the sector-control mode. As it happens this was the preferred mode of operation, which involved transmitting radar waves only over a specified sector of the azimuth circle, thereby minimising the chance of detection by enemy sensors.

MY BAGS ARE IN THE BACK

1500hrs 14th May 1982. A smiling Chief Petty Officer Phillips, as we finished fitting the two vanes. I am lurking somewhere on the other side of the aerial.

The wind-vanes were knocked up in the workshop and attached in a matter of minutes. The aerial rotated as predicted, the picture on the various repeats was perfect and that is how we went to war that night.

0400hrs 15th May 1982 – Naval Gunfire Support for the SAS as they destroy 6 Pucara, 4 Mentor Trainers and 1 SkyVan aircraft.

Unfortunately, after we returned to the UK, someone spotted this picture in a naval article, designed to illustrate the can-do response under difficult conditions and the matter was raised as a question in parliament, on the lines of 'Why were Her Majesty's warships going to war with wind-vanes fitted to their aerials instead of electric motors?'

MY BAGS ARE IN THE BACK

The radar that choked itself to death

After a couple of weeks of the conflict, we suffered a major defect in the ship's main surface and low-level detection radar, the 993 system. This radar was critical in providing detection of surface ships or submarines and more importantly low flying aircraft or missiles. The Extra High Tension (EHT) voltage required to supply the magnetron-like device, the Travelling Wave Tube (TWT), was generated by a large choke and this choke had suffered a massive breakdown in the insulation of the coils around the laminated core. We signalled the other ships in the Task Force to see if anyone had a spare but without luck and soon found that there were no such items available in the UK and that one would have to be manufactured and that this could take a matter of weeks. We were in serious trouble. I contacted all those on board with the technical skill, experience and knowledge of radar systems and the 993 in particular and asked them to meet me in 30 minutes' time with some ideas as to how we might be able to breathe life into the radar.

We met and I looked around the group expectantly. It soon became clear that there was no chance of a miraculous cure by robbing something from a less important system and the situation was adroitly summed up by my most senior radar Chief Petty Officer, in the phrase I had learnt to expect.

"It's totally f...d, Sir."

When they left, I sat there for a while and then went down to the radar office and stared at the offending choke in the base of the power cabinet. It measured about sixteen inches square and seven inches high and comprised a large toroid of laminated magnetic strips surrounded by two inter-connected coils on the two ends of the core. After a few minutes of staring at the damaged section of the coil on the left-hand side, I realised that the right-hand side was completely undamaged. I wondered if we could cut the thick coil wire between the two coils and make use of just the undamaged coil.

I returned to my cabin and thought through the theory. The whole point of the choke was a simple one, namely to provide a charging system to raise the voltage from 440 volts up to the EHT required to drive the TWT, namely many kilovolts. The time taken[15] for a choke to charge to its maximum value is a function of the Inductance and the Resistance in the circuit and if the Inductance is halved, then the time taken to charge up will be halved as well. I could see no reason why the set would not work if the choke got to the correct voltage more quickly, albeit the choke might get rather warm, but we could keep an eye on that.

I asked the Chief for his opinion and after a while we both agreed that we could not see why it wouldn't work and within ten minutes he had the remaining good half of the coil connected as suggested and we stood back as he switched on. The system had a discrete warming-up period while the EHT builds to a stable state, before the voltage is applied to the TWT, and we waited with baited breath until the interlock cut in and the set burst into life and transmitted the energy up the waveguide to the aerial high on the foremast. It worked absolutely brilliantly for the next three weeks until just after the spare unit, shipped from home, had arrived on board. Some members of the operations room staff even suggested that the set worked rather better than before!

---

[15] The Time Constant, which is the time taken to reach 62.3% of full charge is L/R, where L is the inductance and R is the resistance.

The unfortunate Action Stations alarm

It was probably two o'clock in the morning on a "dark and stormy night" and we were one hundred and eighty miles to the east of the Falklands, when the distinctive sound of the Action Stations alarm sounded. The young Principal Warfare Officer (PWO) Lieutenant turned to me, as the senior officer in the Operations Room, gave me a quizzical look and said, "Did you do that, Sir?"

Having replied that I most certainly had not, I suggested that he checked with the Officer of the Watch on the bridge and with the flagship HMS HERMES. We soon established that no one in authority had any reason to sound the alarm. I told the PWO that the only other places where the alarm could be sounded were in HQ1, the damage control centre, in the computer room beneath the Ops Room and lastly on the quarter deck. Having checked with the Ratings in HQ1 and the computer room, and since there was a high sea running, I soon concluded that the probable cause was an ingress of water into the alarm button on the quarterdeck, which was definitely awash.

I turned to the PWO and we agreed that this had been a false alarm and that he should inform the two hundred odd members of the ship's company, who were off watch and who would, by now, be frantically struggling into their action stations clothing. He picked up the main broadcast microphone.

"Do you hear there? This is the PWO in the Ops Room. That was an…"

Having said "an" , I watched with some amusement, I admit, as he struggled to think of an epithet that meant 'false', but of course it had to start with a vowel. After a brief pause he continued, "That was an erroneous alarm."

I should explain that the ship's company had, by now, become well versed in the capability of the French-built Etandard aircraft and its potential to launch the Exocet missile and it was no surprise when two scruffy notices appeared on the ship's company noticeboard, the next morning.

The first one was: "Does an Erroneous carry Exocet?"

The second: "Definition of Erroneous for those of you without a dictionary: 'When you have sh*t yourself unnecessarily'."

The Chinese Laundryman who tried to jump ship

Immediately after the Exocet hit on 12th June, we were in all sorts of trouble and one area of concern was the fact there were two Seaslug missiles on the launcher very close to the fire that was raging in the hangar. We needed to get helicopters on to the flight deck to evacuate the wounded to HMS HERMES and there was a real possibility that the two missiles might be at risk or perhaps endanger the helicopters with their tail rotors a few yards from the launcher. Having sought the Captain's approval and checked we were on a safe bearing, we decided to jettison the missiles by firing them into the sea at a safe range.

Meanwhile one of the Chinese laundrymen[16], Cheung Yu, decided that he had had enough and was going to leave the ship by jumping overboard. The sea was very rough and extremely cold, it was still dark and there was no chance of survival if he had made it. Luckily, the No 1 Chinese laundryman, Chan Lok Wing, had realized that Cheung Yu was in a state of total panic and so chased him as he made his way down 2 deck towards the quarterdeck, where the Seaslug missiles were about to be fired.

In the operations room, having made the final checks, I ordered the Missile Officer to fire both missiles. At this exact moment, Cheung Yu had made his way to the guardrail, right aft on the quarterdeck, immediately below the missile launcher and was trying to get one foot on to the top guardrail to jump into the wake. At this point, Chan Lok Wing had just managed to catch up with Cheung Yu and grabbed him around the thighs in almost perfect rugger tackle. He managed to stop him jumping and started to pull him backwards to the safety of the deck, when the first missile roared past, followed immediately by the other.

---

[16] The team of Chinese contractors had been offered the chance to leave the ship when we came south from Gibraltar, but had decided to remain on board. Apart from the Number One laundryman, Chan Lok Wing, there were six others, a tailor, a shoemaker, three laundrymen and an assistant.

Seaslug firing from HMS GLAMORGAN.

A Seaslug missile weighs in at two tons and by virtue of the four booster rockets, accelerates to Mach 2 almost instantaneously. No one had ever before stood within 100 yards of the flight-path of a Seaslug at launch, but Cheung Yu had now set a new record by being about ten feet from one. Luckily, No 1 laundryman was reasonably protected by Cheung Yu's body and was relatively unharmed, but Cheung Yu was not so fortunate, suffering an immediate loss of hearing as well as losing most of his hair and part of his clothing.

The next day, when things had settled down a bit and the repairs to the damage were well underway, the Captain enquired after Cheung Yu's welfare and suggested that we should invite him to the Captain's cabin for a cup of tea and to ensure that he was being looked after properly. The Captain also suggested that since I had fired the missiles, I should be present. When Chan Lok Wing and Cheung Yu arrived, it is fair to say that the Captain and I were rather apprehensive in case this incident might cause repercussions around the fleet by Chinese laundrymen deciding to seek safer employment.

The Captain and I had decided to create a reasonably relaxed atmosphere and had removed our anti-flash protective headgear and gloves before they were shown in. Before either the Captain or I could even offer the laundrymen a chair, Chan Lok Wing took centre stage.

"Before we start, Sir," he said, "we wish to make statement."

This didn't sound too good, I thought, but nodded and said that we were listening and asked No 1 to continue.

"We have meeting in laundry today and we think Cheung Yu fr...ing idiot. He lose his hearing and his hair because he not wearing his anti-frash."

Poor Cheung Yu, who still could not hear a single thing, saw our broad smiles and our faces portraying a mixture of relief and hilarity, and so he burst out laughing, which got us all going and we then got down to the serious business of tea drinking.

I am very glad to say that Cheung Yu did recover his hearing and his hair grew back.

The Rapier missile system on the hill

When we were hit by the Exocet, we retired to the Tug, Repair and Logistics Area (TRALA) well to the East of the Islands. The staff on board the repair ship, Stena Seaspread, worked wonders repairing the damage to our various weapon systems until we were ready to rejoin the task force, albeit with a slightly reduced capability. However, there was one major problem, which could not be readily solved on the open seas and that was the matter of welding massive steel plates on the main deck where the missile had struck. After several attempts, it became clear that we needed calmer waters if the welding was to be completed. As luck would have it, the Argentinians surrendered on 14th June and on the 18th, we were able to enter San Carlos water and anchor to carry out the repair.

On that day, it was a remarkable feeling to leave the confines of the ship and walk around on the upper deck. For most of us, this was an occasion for many firsts. The first time we had breathed fresh air for many weeks. The first sight of the Falkland Islands. The first daylight we had witnessed. The ship had been 'closed up' for action since well before our first action 1st May and it was a relief after about nine weeks of 'confinement' to relax and stroll around in safety.

One particular Lieutenant Commander, we'll call him 'A', because he is a great friend of mine and I'd like to retain his friendship, was walking down the main deck, past the one remaining un-damaged Seacat missile launcher on the starboard side, when he was approached by one of my lads, a very cheerful and capable Leading Weapon Engineering Mechanic (LWEM).

"Hello Sir," he opened up with, and then asked, "you see those things up on the hill, Sir. What are they then?"

"Those are Rapier missile systems," replied 'A'.

"And how do they work then?" enquired the LWEM.

There was a bit of a pause while the Lieutenant Commander gathered his thoughts.

"Well. You know. It is a missile system and it has some sort of radar system."

18th June 1982 - HMS GLAMORGAN
enters San Carlos water to effect repairs.

The LWEM, who happened to know quite a lot about missiles and radar systems was not over-impressed but thought it best not to pursue the matter and Lieutenant Commander 'A' continued around the upper deck.

A little while later, it was my turn to bump into the same LWEM, who came up to me in his usual cheerful manner.

"I have just a chat with Lieutenant Commander 'A' about those Rapier systems on the hill over there," he volunteered, with a rather downcast look. "A nice chap – not very bright, but a nice chap."

"You can't say that," I spluttered. "He's one of the brightest officers on board and, anyway, you mustn't talk about officers like that."

I was in stitches, really and had to make a hasty retreat. The matter then went downhill later in the day, when I was in the wardroom for a cup of tea and was recounting the sequence of events to some colleagues. I had just got to the final bit about 'A nice chap – not very bright...' when Lieutenant Commander 'A' entered and overheard the final phrase.

Post script. Nine years later, I was serving as a Captain in the Ministry of Defence Main Building in London, when I heard the unmistakable voice of 'A' coming down the corridor outside my office. He and I had not seen each other since late 1982 and 'A' had been promoted twice and had just arrived in London as a newly promoted Captain. We greeted each other warmly and I asked him in and offered him a cup of coffee so that we could catch up on each other's news and exchange those still-vivid memories from April/May/June 1982. As he came into the office and before he even sat down, his very first words were, "Do you think he meant it?"

PPS. I should add that I was proved right about 'A' being 'one of the brightest officers on board' because he went on to be promoted to one of the very highest ranks possible in the Royal Navy and indeed knighted.

The Mexican Commander in the wardroom

When the Argentinians surrendered there was an understandable feeling of relief, mixed with a terrible realisation of the suffering for those at home, whose loved ones had been killed or badly injured. After we had completed the repairs in San Carlos water, we were due to sail for the UK in company with the frigate, HMS PLYMOUTH, also badly damaged, in her case by bombs. As we steamed past HMS HERMES to say farewell and salute her, on the 21st June, we fired a full calibre gun salute from the twin 4.5in guns for'd.

21st June 1982.
We salute HMS HERMES and leave for the UK.

It is difficult to describe the emotion of watching the ship's company of another warship cheer ship as you pass but I can assure you we were all very quiet after the gunfire ceased.

As we steamed north towards warmer weather and calmer seas there was a definite easing of tension and I couldn't resist the temptation to have a bit of fun in the wardroom one evening. We had already removed the deadlights from the ports[17] in those cabins

---

[17] Port, port-hole, scuttle or window, depending on choice.

lucky enough to have one and to look out and see the sea and sky was pure joy, after two months closed up for action. During the conflict the wardroom had been cleared away and transformed ready to act as an operating theatre and clearing station for casualties. Throughout the conflict, therefore, the officers had shared the Senior Ratings' mess aft and now that the war was over, we had moved back into the wardroom, albeit in a limited sense, because the main galley had been virtually destroyed when we were hit and the chefs now had to feed five hundred of us from a galley designed to feed forty-five, and so, for the next three weeks, things were a bit restricted. On that first evening back in the wardroom, I recall looking out of the port, and feeling slightly devilish.

Throughout the conflict I had grown a beard, partly because time between watches was short and sleep, when we had time and were not at actions stations, was at a premium. A few minutes saved were highly valued. Naval traditions have always demanded that permission from the Commanding officer must be sought before growing a beard and of course this I had done many weeks beforehand. It was also required that similar permission should be sought to shave-off. This I had not done. However that evening, I decided that I would shave off 'partly' and leave a definite Mexican-style moustache. In the RN, one can only grow a full beard or none at all and moustaches are totally forbidden.

As one of the five most senior officers on board, I was not in the slightest bit worried about flouting naval tradition for one evening. I set about the task with the scissors and razor and was more than pleased with the effect produced. I went down to the wardroom, expecting that the worst that could possibly happen would be a fine of a round of drinks from the Executive Officer, Commander Chris Gotto.

However, I had underestimated Chris's sense of fun and mischief. The moustache caused a lot of comment, especially from the more junior officers, who certainly did not expect their seniors to behave so boldly and perhaps, badly. Fifteen minutes later and there was a knock on the wardroom door. A young lieutenant approached me and said that the Captain's steward was at the door and wanted to see me. I excused myself from the group I had been talking to and found the steward waiting outside in the flat.

MY BAGS ARE IN THE BACK

25th June 1982. Yours truly - before his come-uppance.

"The Captain wants to see you urgently, Sir," he said.

I needed two or three minutes to shave off the offending moustache and was about to suggest that I was 'still in the shower', when the steward had found me, when he continued: "The Captain said to say that it's really urgent and that I was to bring you back with me immediately. I don't know what it's about, Sir, but I don't think he is taking prisoners on this one."

Blimey, I thought. This sounded serious and so I felt I had no choice but to take the short cut through the empty Captain's quarters adjoining the wardroom and knock on the Admiral's cabin door where the Captain was living.

The look on his face, when he looked up and saw my moustache was a picture and not a pretty one. He looked down again at some papers he was studying and mumbled something like: "I don't wish to know what you think you are doing WEO[18] but I would like to see you back here in five minutes and this time correctly dressed."

I then realised that Chris and the other three Commanders on board had set me up beautifully and dropped me in it with our skipper, Captain Mike Barrow, who knew nothing whatsoever about their clever ruse.

---

[18] Weapon Engineering Officer.

Return to UK

We arrived back in the Channel on 10th July and were due to berth in Portsmouth mid-morning, but had two unexpected visitors off Portland before we got to Spithead.

I was having breakfast when a pipe from the Officer-of-the-Watch on the bridge announced that the frigate HMS SIRIUS, then completing her work-up with Flag Officer Sea Training at Portland prior to deploying to the Falklands, had asked permission to sail close to port to salute us as we returned to British waters. I stood and watched as she approached at speed from the port quarter and was amazed to see that, what appeared to be, the entire the ship's company had turned out and were manning the ship's side from stem to stern. As they passed, they cheered ship and the memory of that sound of three cheers from about 150 fellow sailors still brings a lump to the throat.

The second visitor arrived by helicopter and the ship's company cleared lower deck to be addressed by the Commander-in-Chief-Fleet, Admiral John Fieldhouse[19], who we had last seen 101 days previously, off Gibraltar. Like most senior officers addressing a ship's company, he asked us all to 'gather round' and the four hundred or so GLAMORGANs who were not on watch, did just that, expecting a few words in the form of a brief welcome home. What we got was much more impressive and memorable. He spoke from the heart and although I cannot recall the details, I do remember that he told us how proud he was of what had been achieved by the Task Force and how impressed he had been at the manner in which we had all responded to the demands placed upon us. He went on to warn us that we should be prepared for a fantastic reception in Portsmouth where there were several thousand members of our families waiting in the dockyard and he made it clear that they, like him, had suffered whenever a ship was hit. After speaking for an incredibly emotional ten minutes, he departed. I was intensely moved by this remarkably impressive officer.

---

[19] He was promoted to Admiral of the Fleet on 2 August 1985 and became Chief of the Defence Staff later that month.

HMS SIRIUS - (archive photograph).

We sailed up the Solent, around Spithead and headed for the harbour entrance. The Captain and Executive Officer had agreed that the youngest member of the ship's company, who I believe, was only eighteen, should be standing atop the foremast, 80ft above the sea, so that he could be the first member of the ship's company to see his Mum.

As we approached our berth and saw the vast crowds and the Royal Marine band waiting to welcome us, for the first time since we had sailed south from Gibraltar on 2nd April, I was very emotional.

PETER GALLOWAY

10th July 1982 - The view from the masthead as we approach Portsmouth, after 104 days at sea.

10th July 1982 - Approaching the berth, with the Royal Marine band playing, the crowds cheering and the ship's company waving and trying to spot their families.

Stepping ashore for the first time for over 100 days to meet my family was an amazing feeling and my brother, waiting at our house in Alverstoke, had thoughtfully bought several boxes of smarties, sorted out the green ones, and thrown them all on the lawn for the children to find.

*We set foot ashore for the first time.
Self with my mother, wife, son and daughter.
Dad taking the picture.*

Two days later, I was cycling home to Gosport from the ship, when a car came out of a side road between two dockyard buildings, without appearing to notice or see me and I had to swerve to miss him. The railway lines sunk into the road surface in dockyards are a real hazard to cyclists and this particular railway line caught my front wheel perfectly. I was ejected from the bike and flew in style until I hit the road, when I suffered some abrasions and lost a front tooth. I like to think that the dockyard matey had not seen my accident, but in any case he did not stop, but luckily I was close to a dockyard first aid point and able to get patched up. I did find the irony of the situation somewhat amusing in that I had survived the seven weeks at war, to be taken out by a Pompey dockyard matey.

The ship then entered a lengthy period of maintenance and repair in Portsmouth and during this period we received a visit from the First Sea Lord, Admiral Sir Henry Leach[20]. I was introduced to him, and grateful that I had shaved off the dreadful moustache.

---

[20] Sir Henry was promoted to Admiral of the Fleet in December 1982.

Meeting Sir Henry Leach, First Sea Lord, in the Captain's cabin,
HMS GLAMORGAN.

MY BAGS ARE IN THE BACK

Support from the counties of Glamorgan – The cheque

Throughout the Falklands war, we received fantastic support from the three counties, Mid, South and West Glamorgan and it was therefore essential and appropriate that we should visit the counties to thank those involved. However the damage sustained down south meant that we were to be in Portsmouth dockyard for many months and much as we would have loved to take the destroyer to our Welsh supporters, we had to travel by road.

One of the first visits involved the collection of a cheque for several thousand pounds, raised by a Conservative Association in Barry. As one of the few remaining senior officers still on board GLAMORGAN, following our return to UK, I was selected to travel to Wales to meet the Association's committee one evening, collect the cheque and of course thank them most sincerely. Accompanied by my wife, we drove up from Portsmouth and having settled in to our hotel, we made our way to the venue.

As I walked in, it became clear, from an inspection of the looks on the committee members' faces, that I was not what they were expecting.

"You look so young," said the Chairman of the Association. "We thought a Commodore would look more like Captain Birdseye or something."

I explained that I was a 'Commander' and only thirty-nine, but nevertheless one of the most senior officers on board during the conflict and that I hoped they were not disappointed. After being introduced to the committee members, it was suggested that the cheque be handed over there and then, but that we should repeat the process a bit later on, in front of all of the club members when they assembled in the main hall next door, in thirty minute's time. Having thanked the committee for their very generous cheque, drinks were offered and everyone relaxed.

After half an hour, the Chairman looked at his watch, whispered to one of his colleagues, who promptly disappeared, and turning to me suggested that they were ready for the 'main event'. As he escorted me towards a door, he briefed me.

"Unfortunately, a few of our members won't get here for another quarter of an hour or so, but we've definitely got a quorum. I suppose there are two hundred or so waiting on your every word."

At this point, I may well have looked more than surprised, since no mention of 'main events' or 'words' had been made at any point in the lead up to the evening.

"If you could keep your speech down to about half an hour," he continued, "that would be perfect and that will leave plenty of time for the members to talk to you less formally over a drink or two and perhaps you would like to join in the dancing."

Before I knew it, we were through the door and facing a crowd of clapping members who certainly looked as though they were expecting their money's worth.

No notes. No ideas. Nowhere to hide.

I took a deep breath and decided that the only thing to do was to relive and recount some of the events in the three months, April to June '82. This was the first time I had spoken about the war and I admit that, at times, I became very emotional and occasionally faltered. I spoke for the thirty minutes, as requested, and finished by recounting the extremely moving moment when we berthed in Portsmouth on return to UK and seeing our families on the jetty, and particularly meeting the loved ones of those we had left behind, buried at sea off the Islands.

At this point, I dried up with a rather weak, "Thank you," and stood there. The hall was completely silent for what seemed like an age, no one moved and I felt as though I had committed some sort of terrible mistake. After what was probably only a few seconds, all hell broke loose and the applause was deafening. Moreover, I was practically mobbed by several of the members and I am glad to say that some of them were particularly keen to show their appreciation, especially the young ladies. My wife seems to remember one particular very pretty lady, dressed in a very striking leopard-skin number, but I, of course don't recollect such detail.

The evening was an outstanding success, not so much because of the way the speech was received, but because the Association members realised how their fund-raising efforts and the money they had raised, was going to be put to good use in the South Atlantic Fund.

MY BAGS ARE IN THE BACK

Support from the counties of Glamorgan – The cheers

We, in HMS GLAMORGAN, wanted to visit several places in the three Glamorgan counties that had supported us and there were many invitations from various civic authorities who wanted us to visit their towns or cities and since we could not take the ship, still under repair, eighty of us piled into two coaches and we set off for a three day visit.

We stayed at RAF St Athan and were treated to the most amazing hospitality wherever we went. Unfortunately most people seemed to think that this hospitality should take the form of a reception involving a wide selection of drinks and although this was much appreciated, it made for a long day when the first reception was at 0930 and the final event was a full-blooded dinner dance starting at 2230. I recall, after one particularly testing day, returning to St Athan at about 0300, with two coachloads of, shall we say, 'tired' sailors, who insisted on asking the drivers to stop at the main gate, while they got out, formed an impromptu choir and gave an awful rendition of The Dambusters March, complete with the usual sound effects. Eric Coates would not have been amused and nor was the Group Captain in command of the base, who, next morning invited me as the senior officer, to an interview without coffee in his office.

The next day we were programmed to visit a secondary school, where the children had been writing to the ship and sending us pictures, during the conflict. It was pouring with rain that day and the roads in the valley up the school were flooded and had delayed our arrival by about thirty minutes, which was very annoying since we had been told that the entire school had decided to delay their departure to go home until we arrived. When we eventually got there, all eighty of us were taken quickly to the main assembly hall/gymnasium where the children and staff were waiting and I suppose there were several hundred of them. As we entered, they started cheering and clapping and then broke into song with the most beautiful rendition of 'Congratulations' and as the voices echoed around the room, it was extremely emotional.

We were invited to move amongst the children and before long we were chatting away and signing autographs. The buses waiting to take the children were now running so late that the children had to start boarding and so the crowd started to thin out. As I was signing a few last autographs, I noticed one particular girl, of about thirteen, who was clearly upset and standing back from the rest of the group. Finally, she stood alone, and I could see that it was all too much for her as the tears started to form. At this point I was very concerned in case she had suffered some family loss during the war, perhaps within the Welsh Guards on board the Sir Galahad. I leant down and said how sorry I was that she was crying and asked what was wrong. In the most lovely Welsh accent, she looked up at me, through the tears, "I just think you're sooooo brave," and off she ran to catch her bus.

Support from the counties of Glamorgan – The cheeky

We also visited a junior school, where the children had been writing to us down south and sending us small parcels and after a general chat with the staff and all of the children, a small group of us were led away to be taken singly to a classroom each, for the children to have time for personal questions.

I was invited to a classroom, asked to sit at the front, while the female teacher, took her place at the back of the class.

"Alright, Jimmy," she said, "you wanted to ask the first question. Off you go then."

Jimmy was about ten years old and he stood up, smartly and confidently.

"Commander," he said, and I thought, 'Hmm, he's off to a good start.'

"What was the first thing you did to your wife when you got home?"

I glared at the teacher who was desperately trying to leave the room via the window at the back.

"I gave her a kiss, Jimmy," said I, and felt pretty confident that I had handled that one rather well.

"Yes, I know that," replied Jimmy with a smirk. "But what did you do after that?"

The Welsh Guards Major comes visiting

During the Falklands war, a Welsh Guards officer, Major Griffiths-Eton, was ashore on the islands involved in the final push for Stanley on 12th June and witnessed the tragic moment when the Exocet missile hit GLAMORGAN. He later explained that the explosion and bright flash, in the darkness of the early morning, was so vivid that he could not believe a ship could survive. He was particularly upset because he knew that GLAMORGAN had been supplying extensive Naval Gunfire Support to the Welsh Guards and other units as they advanced towards Stanley.

Months passed, the ship had returned to UK, undergone extensive repair work and eventually returned to join the fleet. On a visit to Gibraltar, some of the officers were invited by the Adjutant of the resident Army regiment on the rock to a drink in their mess, and even more delighted when we met the Major and he recounted how upset he had been when he saw the 'Welsh' destroyer hit and how pleased he was to see us back in service. We invited him back to the ship on the following evening.

The Major arrived in civilian clothes and was met at the top of the gangway by the Officer of the Day, who happened to be one of my section officers. The Major raised his trilby, stood smartly to attention and addressed the Lieutenant.

"Good evening. Major Griffiths Eton."

My Lieutenant saluted.

"Good evening, Sir," he replied, "Lieutenant Mills, Turves Green Secondary Modern."

I still don't know whether Mills was taking the proverbial.

MY BAGS ARE IN THE BACK

Put the Commander's bed out will you

In mid-November 1983, whilst GLAMORGAN was still in Gibraltar, the members of the ship's company, who were ashore, were surprised when a general recall was issued and the naval patrol toured the rock to spread the word. The British government was concerned that the UK element of the Multinational Force in the Lebanon, Her Majesty's 1st The Queen's Dragoon Guards might need some support, since the situation with the various warring factions was deteriorating. GLAMORGAN and the frigate HMS BRAZEN were to make haste, in company with the RFA BLUE ROVER providing the replenishment at sea capability on the way down the Mediterranean, to stand off the Lebanese coast. The situation in Beirut was extremely dangerous following the bombing of the Beirut barracks on 23rd October, when a suicide bomber drove a truck packed with explosives into the U.S. Marine barracks in Beirut, killing 241 U.S. military personnel. That same morning, 58 French soldiers were killed in their barracks two miles away in a separate suicide terrorist attack.

It soon became clear that one way in which we could help the Dragoon Guards would be to take small groups at a time away from the deprivation and dangers in their tobacco-factory base on the ground in Beirut. The two factions, the Christians and Muslims, were in the habit of exchanging fire using RPGs, on a regular basis at sunset, across the waste ground in front of the tobacco factory where the Dragoons were based. We had embarked an additional RN Commander, who was to land and be embedded with the Dragoons to act as our point of liaison for the duration of our tour of duty.

On his first afternoon ashore with the Guards, he later related, he was shown to his accommodation comprising a small bare room with a bunk bed, one opening in the concrete-block walls acting as a window space and a bunk bed. The view through the 'window' was unusual in that it was partially obscured by the protective anti-RPG nets that the Dragoons had hung from the roof of the building. He dropped his kit off and left his beret in the middle of the bunk bed and toured the facilities offered by the tobacco factory in the company of the Lieutenant Colonel in command. At about ten minutes to six, on that first evening, the Colonel suggested they take a stroll up to the roof to watch the firefight.

"It always starts at 1800 and it is usually quite good fun," said the colonel.

Sure enough, at 1800, the rounds started streaking across the waste ground in both directions and remarkably close to the factory. The Lt Colonel seemed remarkably relaxed about the whole thing, even when one RPG was clearly 'inbound'. It struck the factory nets somewhere below them and detonated with a crack and a roar. After a while, the firings ceased and they descended to assess the damage. By chance the round had tried to enter the building through the Commander's window, but the net had done its job. As the Colonel and Commander walked pass, they saw that the jet of flame from the RPG had managed to reach several yards into the room and had set fire to the Commanders beret and his bedding. The Colonel turned to the Corporal accompanying them.

"Put the Commander's bed out, will you, Corporal," he said and they continued down to the ground floor.

The next phase of this remarkable day for the Commander was when he heard the Colonel instructing his Sergeant to get some transport sorted out because he was going to go over to the blighters who had fired that particular round and sort them out. That is exactly what ensued and when they arrived at the Muslim faction's base, a couple of hundred metres away, he was received by the 'commander' with considerable respect. The situation was discussed and the Lt Colonel expressed his displeasure. At this there was an exchange of Arabic and a man was despatched, to return a few minutes later with a sadly dejected-looking combatant. The 'commander" interrogated him for a few moments and when the poor unfortunate nodded and mumbled what was clearly in the affirmative, the 'commander' drew his pistol and pistol-whipped him, twice.

The British duo returned to their base, hoping that the number of RPG strikes would diminish.

A flight into Beirut

For a couple of weeks, we had used the Lynx helicopter to extract groups of the Dragoon Guards for periods of twenty-four hours to give them a break from the shore-side routine, to give them a chance to have a good wash and brush up and to give them the best square meals we could provide. It was then suggested that we should host a meeting, on board GLAMORGAN, of the Dragoons' Commanding Officer, our own Captain and the Ambassador Extraordinary and Plenipotentiary at Beirut, Sir David Miers (I believe).

The Lynx was to collect the Ambassador and his Military Attaché and apart from the pilot and the observer, there was a requirement for someone to act as shotgun in case of an incident on the route, which was known to be hazardous in the extreme. The threats were from small arms, RPGs and worst of all from virtually invisible wires stretched across the wadis in which the helicopter was to fly through the centre of Beirut. I asked if I could go along as shotgun and was handed the sterling and a few magazines. As I made my way towards the Lynx, with the crew, the pilot grinned and said he thought it might be safer for everyone if he had the magazines up front with him. Overcoming the cheek of the pilot, I took my place in the back, which was stripped of unnecessary equipment, including both doors. Having ensured that I was safely secured to the helicopter floor, with a wire lanyard, we set off.

We flew past the US battleship, New Jersey, providing Naval Gunfire Support, flat out across the sea towards the city at about twenty feet and within minutes popped up as the city limits flew beneath us.

The pilot who had clearly done all this many times found the main drainage wadi, which was a concrete structure, not much wider than our rotor blades and we flew so low, to avoid RPG attack, that at times the blades were level with the roads on the side of the wadi. All eyes were looking ahead for the dreaded wires across the wadi and I took this photograph as we popped up to get over the bridge ahead.

Figure 11983 - Standing off Beirut.
The US Battleship, New Jersey, gathers speed as we steam close by.

Flying in the wadi in Beirut.
We pop up as the pilot decides not to attempt flying under the bridge ahead.

MY BAGS ARE IN THE BACK

The next and extremely exciting manoeuvre came as we flew at about eighty knots towards the next wadi, which involved a right-angled turn to port. I am still not quite sure what happened next but I do recall wondering what was holding us up as I saw that we had rolled more than 90° as we turned, but reassured myself by presuming that the tail rotor must be providing some element of lift.

The final manoeuvre in this frenetic flight involved flying fast towards the only vertical-sided hill I could see in Beirut, until we were practically hitting the rocky side, when the pilot applied maximum collective and revs and we shot up some three hundred feet and landed on a grassy area, which had once been a football pitch. The Ambassador, the Military Attaché and the Lieutenant Colonel commanding the Dragoons, accompanied by a couple of protection officers, were assembled and the trio for the meeting were hurried on board and strapped in behind me in the rear of the cabin in seconds and we were off.

The Lynx landing on the football pitch, Beirut.

The first few seconds of flight included the three hundred foot drop over the side of the precipice. It was more than exhilarating and I turned to check the Ambassador was OK. He looked distinctly green and I reached for the brown paper bags that the pilot had said we might well need. As we re-entered the first wadi, things looked even worse behind me and I passed the bags to the Attaché. The

Ambassador grabbed for a bag as we completed the turn into the second wadi and I averted my eyes. We were back on board GLAMORGAN within eight minutes and I helped the Ambassador onto the flightdeck, whilst relieving him of his bag.

I changed back into uniform for the lunch in the Admiral's cabin and joined the Captain, the other Heads of Department and our VIP guests. The Captain, who was not aware that I had been flying that morning, introduced me to the Ambassador, who looked at me quizzically.

"Have we met before?" he said with a puzzled frown.

"I am sure I would have remembered if we had," I replied.

The lunch was a business-like affair and one topic concerned the fairly primitive living conditions that the army troops ashore were enduring. When it came to speeches, the usual votes of thanks were proffered for this and that and our Captain then asked the Dragoons Lieutenant Colonel whether there was anything in particular that the Royal Navy could provide to assist their hard-pressed Army colleagues ashore.

"A crate of this very decent port would go down well in the officers' mess," replied the Colonel.

1984/86 - MOD, NAVAL SECRETARY, WEAPON ENGINEERING APPOINTER

The Naval Secretary and his staff were accommodated in one of the most historically interesting buildings in London, part of the Old Admiralty Building in Whitehall. The present building was designed by the Master Carpenter, Thomas Ripley, and completed in 1726 (at an "Expense that hath very much exceeded the Estimate"), becoming known as Ripley Block. The building contains the room where Nelson's body lay overnight on 8th/9th January 1806, before his funeral. It also contains the Admiralty Board Room, a survivor from the original building of 1695, with its finely carved over-mantel, attributed to Grinling Gibbons' workshop, depicting ancient nautical instruments. The Board Room boasts an imposing table, with a cut out portion to accommodate the Secretary and his papers. The wind dial, controlled by a vane on the roof, and the carving have survived from the 1695 building. The room was expertly repaired after being damaged by a bomb in World War Two.

From here, the worldwide affairs of the Royal Navy were run for centuries by "the Lords' Commissioners of the Admiralty" until they were replaced, on the formation of the Ministry of Defence in 1964, by the "Admiralty Board of the Defence Council" . The board still occasionally meets in the Old Admiralty Board Room.

My office, on the ground floor, faced onto the impressive courtyard on Whitehall and here I was responsible, under the Director, for appointing the Weapon Engineer Commanders and also the more senior Lieutenant Commanders who were 'in-zone' for promotion, some four hundred in all. It was an amazingly satisfying job, albeit, it carried with it some aspects which I had not foreseen. Since one was intimately involved in arranging appointments for those junior and senior to oneself as well as one's peers, a certain amount of tact and diplomacy was required, especially when attempting to fit a square peg into the proverbial round hole.

The day that the American Secretary of State came to lunch

In the corner of the Ripley Block courtyard is the main entrance to a relatively unknown building, Admiralty House, designed by Samuel Pepys Cockerell, a protégé of Sir Robert Taylor, and opened in 1788. Built at the request of Admiral of the Fleet Viscount Howe, First Lord of the Admiralty, in 1782–83 for "a few small rooms of my own" , it was the official residence of First Lords of the Admiralty until 1964, and has also been home to several British Prime Ministers when 10 Downing Street was being renovated. The U.S. President John F. Kennedy attended a meeting there with Prime Minister Harold Macmillan in 1962 to discuss the allies' reaction to the communist threat and more wide-ranging matters. Winston Churchill lived in the house while serving as First Lord of the Admiralty for two terms, 1911–15 and 1939-40.

During my time in Ripley Block it contained government function rooms and three ministerial flats but the accommodation, particularly the main reception rooms were outstandingly well appointed. It was in the dining room of Admiralty House, that the British government were going to host a luncheon for the visiting American Secretary of State, George P Shultz. As the morning of the lunch passed, I noticed that the courtyard was slowly but surely filling up with large black American-plated cars, until by midday, the entire courtyard was jammed full with scarcely room to walk through from Whitehall to Admiralty House or indeed to Ripley Block. Soon, the various drivers, all of whom appeared to be exact genetic clones and identically suited, took station in a geometric grid throughout the courtyard and then, one by one, at intervals of exactly one minute, they would stick a finger into their left ear. Then they would speak a few words, remove the finger from the ear and start surveying the courtyard and each other. This process was repeated for every one of the twelve 'Government Men' until, after several repetitions, I lost interest and got back to work.

Some time later I heard a car start up and looking out again, I saw that the car nearest to Whitehall and the one lined up with the narrow entrance was leaving. Clearly, they were preparing for the arrival of the car containing George P Shultz. Nothing happened however and the G-men resumed their monotonous earwax removal routine. Just as I was about to look away, all twelve of them simultaneously adopted the finger-in-the-ear pose, jaws dropped and their faces displayed a complex mixture of concern, consternation and disbelief, as they swivelled to face the entrance. At that point, I honestly thought that the Secretary of State had decided to fool them all and had decided to walk to Admiralty House and was about to be assaulted, or worse, by a would-be assassin as he entered the courtyard. This was a very serious situation and the G-men were, by now, all talking into their invisible microphones, but strangely no one was moving.

The window in my office faced the entrance to Admiralty House across the courtyard and I was unable to see the pedestrian gateway into the courtyard and so was unaware of the cause of this extremely serious crisis. The tension was palpable but slowly all was revealed and the looks of disbelief on the G-men were replaced by looks of astonishment, then amusement and finally back to disbelief.

At that time, there was a very distinctive female member of staff working in the manpower and Training Directorate. She was well over six feet tall, extremely beautiful, with a stunning figure and the most amazingly well developed bust. The weather that day was particularly warm and sunny and she had chosen an outfit that certainly displayed her undoubted assets to the world at large. As she wended her way through the parked cars and past the G-men, who followed her every step, towards the entrance to Ripley Block, there is no doubt in my mind, that if Mister Shultz had chosen to arrive at that moment, his security would very definitely have been at risk.

The senior submarine Commander and his final appointment

Whereas more junior officers were given their appointments without too much in the way of discussion, in-zone Lieutenant Commanders and Commanders were very definitely involved in the process of agreeing on their next appointment, even if the final result was not always to their entire satisfaction. On one occasion I was waiting to see a Commander, several years senior to me, who was coming to the end of his naval career and about to get his final appointment in the service. I had done my homework on his background and his stated preferences for types of appointment and felt confident that I would be able to offer him a particularly attractive appointment, which certainly reflected well on his experience and seniority.

This officer, being a submariner, had spent a lot of his recent working life in Scotland in the submarine base and with his family home in Plymouth, I had identified an eminently suitable appointment there, which I felt that both he and his wife deserved, after a very successful career.

As a general service officer, I had had little contact with the submarine service, and I had never bumped into this particular Commander and I was determined to do the best for him, particularly because my immediate boss was an eminent submarine Captain and he had already suggested that my relief, when it was my turn to move on, should be a submariner to balance things up.

The normal process, when discussing the way ahead for an officer was to table at least three options for consideration, all of which were chosen to suit his stated preferences. In this case, I was so convinced that he would jump at the appointment in Plymouth, that I had nothing else on the list. The Commander arrived in my office as planned and we chatted for a few minutes before I got round to the matter in hand. I stressed how his considerable experience and seniority was exactly what the Plymouth set-up needed and that I knew that the Admiral and his prospective boss, the Captain concerned, would be delighted.

There was a very definite pause. The Commander appeared to be less than impressed.

"Is there a problem?" I enquired.

"The truth of the matter," he replied, "is that my wife and I haven't lived together for the last ten years and I'm not sure either of us are quite ready for it just yet. Is there any chance I could stay in Faslane?"

We settled down to investigate what was available and eventually identified another opportunity and he went on his way much happier.

An interview without coffee for a colleague

One summer, we all agreed that it would be good to have a dinner for all the Appointers within the Directorate, together with our wives, and we booked a table at the Les Routier restaurant at Camden Lock, NW1. The party was led by our Director, a senior submariner Captain, and he and his wife were joined by four Commanders, three Lieutenant Commanders and the wives. The evening was a pleasant summery event with excellent food and wine and all was proceeding smoothly until an itinerant lady entered the restaurant, selling single roses.

One of our group, yes it was me, foolishly fell for the sales technique and bought one, at an exorbitant price, for his wife. Groans followed as others in the group felt pressurised to do the same for their wives. Eventually, the gypsy lady moved on to the next gullible table, smiling broadly.

As she left us, one of the other Commanders, John, noticed that the Director, the senior submarine Captain, had not fallen for the ruse and his wife was left rose-less. John was sitting next to the Captain's wife at one end of the table and adjacent to one of the many open windows onto the canal. Each window was adorned, on the outside, with a suitable barge-painted window box and as I recall, the one next to John's window contained geraniums. In an act of inexcusable vandalism and without moving from his chair, he thrust his arm through the open window, grabbed a handful of stalks and presented them to the Captain's wife, the earth from the roots spilling onto the table and her plate.

"Because your husband…" he exclaimed, in a slightly slurred but nevertheless loud voice, "…is so (bleeped) miserable, I have got you this beautiful bouquet of flowers."

An enormous silence descended on the table and settled like a dense fog as eyes turned towards the Captain. One eyebrow was raised ever so slightly, and he diverted his stare from John and continued his conversation with those next to him. I should add that the Captain's wife was, at this stage, wearing a smile almost as broad as the departed gypsy, although I am not sure whether this was to indicate her pleasure at being presented with the flowers or at her husband's discomfort.

The dinner was, otherwise, an enormously successful event and we returned to work the next morning feeling thoroughly satisfied that we had achieved the aim of establishing a friendly and cheerful working environment in the Directorate. Almost immediately, John received a summons to the Director's office and you've already guessed what ensued – an interview without coffee.

Lunch at Simpson's-in-the-Strand and the unexpected consequence

I was about to interview a Lieutenant-Commander, David, a contemporary of mine and a good friend, who had unfortunately failed to be promoted to Commander and was coming to see me to discuss his next and final job. He was a specialist in the world of satellite communications and there were very limited opportunities for him, especially if I was to make best use of his experience.

We talked through the various jobs that I had identified and there was a definite lack of enthusiasm for almost everything on the plot. He suddenly looked at his watch and exclaimed, "Goodness. Look at the time. We'd better get a move on. I've booked a table for us at Simpson's-in-the-Strand at one o'clock and we're going to be late."

This splendid idea was all news to me and when he added that it was 'all on him' I was more than impressed. As we strolled down the Strand, I smiled and turning to David, pointed out that this splendid lunch was not going to affect the outcome of what appointments were available. We both laughed and agreed to change the subject and let David have a couple of weeks to consider the way ahead and the possibilities we had discussed.

The lunch was marvellous and the roast meat on silver-domed trolleys, carved at the table in the 1828 oak-panelled dining room, was outstanding. When we walked back to Whitehall, David carried on to the Main Building as I entered Old Admiralty Building. I was a little downcast to think that I couldn't give David a really interesting job as he came to the end of his career, but realised that I was not a magician.

Thirty minutes later, the telephone rang and an Admiral in the Main Building, who I did not know, was on the line.

"I have just been speaking to The Naval Secretary," he barked. "He tells me that you're the chap who can solve my problem. I need a Commander for a very important post in my organisation on Monday morning. He must be a satellite communications expert, and I mean expert. Got it?"

"Yes, Sir, I understand the problem, but I can tell you straight away that there are only a handful of such animals and they are very much in demand and totally committed at the moment."

"That's your problem," he retorted, "and it is your job to find a solution. This is a real priority and your Admiral, the Naval Secretary, has already said that you will be able to provide someone."

"The only solution," I replied, "would be for the Naval Secretary to sanction promoting a Lieutenant-Commander on an acting basis, and I happen to know that there is a moratorium on that at the moment."

"Don't worry about that," replied the Admiral, "you find me an officer and I'll fix the Naval Secretary and his moratorium."

He rang off and I immediately thought of the only officer on my plot, who could possibly fill the bill. David. At this stage, it is worth pointing out that a Lieutenant-Commander who held the rank of Acting-Commander for at least one year was entitled to a Commander's pension and the step up to this pension was very considerable, the rank of Commander being seen as the first of the 'senior officer' ranks.

I picked up the telephone and rang David and started by thanking him for the splendid lunch and then asked him if he would be happy to consider another opportunity which had literally arisen in the last few minutes, but it would mean another three-year stint in London if he accepted. I explained the job specification and finally pointed out that he would have to have his uniform altered to reflect his rank as a Commander. There was a pause and then he replied, "Are you saying that every Lieutenant-Commander who takes you out to lunch gets promoted?"

I am pleased to say that he did get the promotion and indeed stayed there for a full tour and quite rightly received the increased pension.

1986/87 - THE ADMIRALTY INTERVIEW BOARD (AIB)

Having attended the AIB as a schoolboy, it was intriguing to be appointed there as a Member of the Board in 1986 and to witness the exhaustive testing of each candidate during the three-day process. During my appointment, I was promoted to Captain and so spent the first six months as the Commander on one of the Boards and then a further six months as a Captain and the President of a Board. The practical tests, designed to explore the candidate's leadership skills, their initiative and power of command were carried out in a large aeroplane hangar and provided the opportunity for some amusing moments. The tasks involved a group of four or five candidates, each one being asked to lead a challenge set by the staff in the hangar. Tasks might involve the whole team crossing a 'ravine' of twenty feet from one platform on a gym mat to another using ropes, spars, planks and 40-gallon oil drums, whilst carrying a load of some description. Other tasks embodied a water hazard several feet deep, which, if nothing else, raised the prospect of an early bath if things went wrong.

A histrionic effect echoed around the hangar

While still a Commander, I was watching and marking the members of a team of five candidates in their practical task in the hangar. One particular candidate had been asked by his team leader to shin up a spar from the starting platform to a loop in a rope at the centre of the 'ravine' some ten feet away. The spar was inclined at twenty degrees and the climb obviously involved a certain amount of effort as he pulled himself up foot by foot. About halfway up the spar, the effort being exerted by the candidate was obviously just a bit too much and this caused a histrionic effect, much amplified by the acoustics of the metal hangar.

Whilst the rest of his team tried to supress their giggles, the candidate on the spar retained his composure, looked over his shoulder and addressed his team leader, "Sorry about that," he calmly announced.

He went on to pass the whole examination process with ease, which was not a particular surprise, since his distinguished public school had already spotted his potential by selecting him as head boy, and he was certain to be given a place as a Cadet at BRNC Dartmouth when he left school. However we were to see this candidate some time later, when his Careers Adviser at school, suggested that perhaps he should attend the AIB again with a view to getting a Scholarship entry to the College. Accordingly, he reappeared some months later, by which time I was a Captain and the President of his Board.

When the five candidates had been briefed by the staff of Senior and Junior Ratings in the hangar, prior to their practical tasks, the President of the Board would be introduced to the candidates and a few encouraging words exchanged. Most candidates would, at this stage, be nervous and withdrawn. Not this particular candidate, however. When I reached him, he not only recognised me, but he congratulated me on my promotion and then grinned.

"Don't worry Sir," he said, "I left out the baked beans at breakfast this morning."

Again, he passed with distinction.

A candidate has a nasty fall

One practical leadership task involved a candidate being asked by his team leader to swing on a rope to the centre of the 'ravine' and reach a spar suspended between two ropes hanging from the roof of the hangar. This he managed and the four Members of the Board were suitably impressed and noted his skill, particularly because he was a small and fairly skinny young man. The leader then wanted to pass a fifteen-foot plank to the centre of the spar and so asked the candidate in the middle of the ravine to make his way to the centre of the spar by sliding along it. This struck us all as a tricky manoeuvre that might end in tears, but the candidate set off and we held our breath, as he wobbled his way along.

The tasks were against the clock and time was definitely running out as he made his way along and the rest of the team encouraged him lustily. He reached the centre of the spar and we were again impressed, but nevertheless were concerned, as his position appeared precarious in the extreme. It was then that Board Members and the hangar staff, overseeing the task, exchanged a few looks. Unfortunately, the candidate did look as though he was making a surprisingly good impression of a parrot sitting on a perch. He continued to wobble and we realised that until the plank arrived, he was in danger of falling. Our attention was then drawn to the rest of the team as they struggled to pass the long and heavy plank to the man on the spar. Suddenly there was a thump from the ravine and we turned to see that the candidate had fallen the two feet onto the gym mats in the middle of the ravine.

"I'm sorry," he said, addressing his team leader, in a nervous, high-pitched squeak.

Normally a candidate would have to return to the starting platform and try again, but time was running out and the Petty Officer on the hangar staff, responsible for the candidates' safety, quite correctly looked at his stopwatch and turned to me.

"Shall I put him back on his perch, Sir?"

I regret to say we all had to turn away and pretend to make copious notes on our clipboards.

1988 - NATIONAL DEFENCE COLLEGE, NEW DELHI

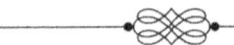

In 1959, following a visit to the Royal College of Defence Studies in Belgrave Square, Pandit Jawaharlal Nehru, the first prime minister of independent India, sanctioned the setting up of a National Defence College for providing instruction to senior service and civil service officers in the wider aspects of higher direction and strategy of warfare. The building chosen to house the College was the erstwhile British High Commission that had relocated to the Diplomatic Enclave in Chanakyapuri, New Delhi, an area established to house all of the other Embassies and High Commissions.

I joined the 28th course at the NDC, lasting eleven months, in January 1988, together with 50 Indian service and civilian officers and 22 Foreign Service officers.

The National Defence College, New Delhi.

The National Defence College building was originally the British High Commission until a replacement site was established in the Diplomatic Enclave in Chankyapuri in the 1950s. It is in Tees January Marg (30th January Street) and is facing the house now known as Ghandi Smriti. This was the house where Gandhi spent the last 144 days of his life until his assassination on 30 January 1948. The house, owned originally by the Birla family, Indian business tycoons, and formerly known as Birla House or Birla Bhavan, is now a museum dedicated to Gandhi.

Day One in India - Clearing Customs

Lynn and I had no diplomatic status for our year in India but the British High Commission in India did help us enormously and on our first full day, the High Commission provided me with a Locally Employed member of the Administration department, Raju, to help me through the process of clearing our personal possessions through customs at the Indira Ghandi International Airport.

When appointed to the NDC, one is given plenty of advice and specific instructions on how to pack your clothes, electronic equipment, white goods, crockery and so on. Everything had to be crated, clearly marked with crate number, owner, destination and finally a detailed list of contents and prices. It was also stated that everything had, most unusually, to be segregated specifically so that the electronic equipment could be readily identified. In the UK we couldn't really understand the need for this attention to detail, but all was about to become clear as we approached the vast customs hangar at the airport.

Although January, the hangar was dusty and warm at 0900 and we were escorted to our twenty-four crates. The customs 'inspector' turned out to be a rather ordinary man with a large jemmy bar and very little else to commend him for handling our prized possessions. Luckily, we had been told to take a cordless screwdriver with us to remove the twelve screws securing each wooden lid, and persuaded him to put the jemmy away.

The first crate he wanted to inspect was clothing and by chance (I wonder) he chose a crate containing some of my wife's clothes. Having been asked to remove the lid of the second crate, I started work with the screwdriver and some moments later checked how he was getting on, to find him rummaging around in the depths of the crate, to find and extract her underwear, which he then held up and sniffed! That was it. I grabbed the jemmy and demanded in fluent Hindi, which I couldn't speak, that he be replaced immediately.

Things proceeded more serenely after he had gone and the next 'inspector' was, at least, not a deviate and the pile of crate lids on the hangar floor grew throughout the day. Finally we got to the crates with the electronics and at this the 'inspector' was replaced by another, and this one was wearing a uniform rather than a pair of overalls. The procedure now involved every single item being removed from the crates, unwrapped from the bubble wrap and then inspected. At this point I was asked for my passport and he found an empty page and stamped it with a full-page stamp bearing the Indian Customs logo and lots of dotted lines. He inspected the television and asked me for the serial number, which he recorded in the passport. This was repeated for everything with an electrical lead attached, until I couldn't contain my curiosity any longer.

"Why are you writing the serial numbers in the passport?"

"That is to ensure that when you leave India," he solemnly replied, "we can check that you have not sold any of these valuable items and undermined the indigenous market for Indian goods."

'Oh well,' thought I and opened another crate. All went well until he discovered a small battery charger with an electric lead, which he was clearly confused by.

"What is this?"

"A battery charger for re-chargeable batteries," I replied.

"Serial number please."

I searched and unsurprisingly, none was to be seen.

"There isn't one," I said.

"I'll have to confiscate it then, I'm afraid."

I looked again for the missing serial number and declared with a certain air of triumph, "Here it is. Write this number down in the passport. '220V AC'"

He did and it remained in my passport for evermore.

Unfortunately that was not the end of the saga. At about 1645, we had finished the inspection process and so I turned to Raju and asked, "So what now?"

"Simple. The Customs Chief Inspector will work out the duty payable on the goods you are importing based on the prices you stated on the contents list."

Ten minutes later and I was presented with a bill for something like 300,000 Rupees, which in those days was about £6,000. Needless to say, I didn't have that much on me, or even in the bank.

"They are joking, of course," I said, but was told not to worry as we could probably come to 'some arrangement'. We traipsed back to see the Chief Inspector and after a few minutes, it was agreed that the duty payable was amended to Rs 600 or about £12. That amount I could handle. With some relief, we were directed to the other end of the hangar to pay at the cashier's window. It was now 5pm exactly and as I got to within 5 feet of the window, it closed. I knocked and the shutter slid up.

"Yes?"

"Good evening. I have come to settle up."

"We're closed. You'll have to come back tomorrow at 0900."

I could not believe that after eight hot, dusty, frustrating hours, we were two seconds late. I discussed the situation for another minute or two but realised that I was not going to win when the cashier told me, and I had to believe him didn't I, that the till was on a time-lock to prevent fraud and corruption. That was the last straw. We came back the next day.

How to make ice cubes in India

We were given a small but delightful bungalow in West End Colony for the course, an extremely desirable area in New Delhi, with an equally small but adequate garden. The staff comprised a bearer, a cook, a gardener and three chowkidars[21]. The bearer, James was a Christian, whose son Jordan was one of the chowkidars who lived with his wife Mary in a small but pleasant flat at the rear of the bungalow. James and his family were Christians who had served the British NDC student for many years in the same property.

James was quite a character. One day he laughed when he found Lynn standing on a chair in the sitting room one day, as a small mouse ran across the room.

"What are you laughing at James?" shrieked Lynn. "Do something!"

"Sorry Memsahib. But the mouse always living that chair. Last Memsahib stand on sofa, the year before Memsahib run out door. Every Memsahib do something different."

We had been warned to take care with our health and particularly with the risk of amoebic dysentery with salads, washing vegetables and with ice cubes. One day as I was passing the kitchen, I saw James wrestling with the ice-cube tray, which was refusing to release the next batch of ice-cubes into the ice bucket for a round of drinks. I watched as he struggled, until giving up, he did what anyone would do in the UK, namely he put the tray under the tap. There's a short cut to dysentery, I thought.

"James. What are you doing?"

He reached for his false teeth, which were resting on the top of the fridge-freezer, inserted them and gave me a look as though I must surely know how to get reluctant cubes out of a tray and replied, "Sahib. If you run water over the ice-cubes, they come out pretty damned quick."

"James," I said, "tell me how you make ice-cubes."

---

[21] Property watchman.

Another withering look came my way that seemed to convey that he could not believe that Captains in the Royal Navy did not know how to make ice-cubes.

"I am boiling the water for 20 minutes and then letting to cool, before putting into tray and freezing, Sahib."

"There's no need to boil for twenty minutes," I said, "let's agree on three minutes, shall we? But why do you think we boil the water at all, James?"

"Sahib. I am working here for many years and plenty different Sahibs, but no one ever explain that bit. Is it something religious?"

The day the front door caught fire

The weather in Delhi is such that receptions can be held outdoors for eight or nine months of the year and we had every excuse to entertain fellow students. The first such garden reception went well but I had been disappointed with the number of lights used to adorn the various trees. In India, they use necklaces of lights on the main 220-volt supply and with guaranteed dry conditions there is little reason to worry about a short-circuit.

While planning for the second such reception, I asked James, the bearer, to ensure we had a 'lot more' lights. On the evening of the party, I went out to see the garden ablaze with lights and James with the widest smile imaginable. I noticed that there were an awful lot of wires leading to a single 13 Amp socket at the side of the house and that they were jammed into the socket with matchsticks. I leant down to check it was not overheating. Everything seemed fine and the reception went ahead without a hitch.

My daughter, then seventeen, came running up to me an hour later.

"Dad, Dad, you'd better come quickly. The front door's on fire."

Sure enough, as I went into the bungalow, I could smell burning wood and there was the door, with the electrical fuse panel leaning against it, having been blown off the adjacent wall.

Flames were licking up the door as I spotted the bearer, James, charging from the kitchen with a saucepan of water determined to electrocute himself, and possibly others, by throwing water onto the 220-volt fuse panel. Instead, I opened the main breaker for the house and we extinguished the fire with a fire blanket.

As a student at the NDC, I had no diplomatic status, of course, but the British High Commission looked after us throughout the year and on this occasion, late in the evening, I rang and asked for assistance to restore power and within minutes they arrived, stuck the fuse panel back on the wall, inserted the traditional six-inch nails in as fuses and we carried on with the party.

'Elth and Safety' eat your heart out.

The exploding radiogram

One of the interesting features of life in New Delhi concerned the supply of mains electricity. Unlike the UK where each house is supplied with electricity using one single phase of the three phases supplied by the generators at the power station, in India, each house is supplied with all three phases and they are distributed around the house to spread the load equally across all three. This could mean that in one room the light in one corner would be on the red phase, the ceiling light on yellow and the television on the blue. Unfortunately there is one other problem with the supply and that is that it's remarkably unstable and fluctuates wildly as consumers switch devices on and off. This can result in extreme cases in the most amazing scenes as the standard light flares from a 60 watt effect to 150 watt, as the television fades away to nothing and the table lamp flickers before deciding to explode.

However all is not lost since devices do exist to protect the sensitive devices such as the electronic equipment and the television, for instance, which would be connected via a Surge Suppressor. Unfortunately we were only supplied with a limited number and on one particular evening the old-fashioned radiogram suffered, as a massive surge threw the room into a series of alternating dark and bright lights in different corners. Finally the radiogram started to emit smoke and before we could reach it, expired with a loud crack.

On inspection, it was clear that the mains transformer had been unable to resist the enormous peak in voltage and was a burnt-out wreck. Reluctant to condemn the device to the tip and being very much aware of the Indian ability to mend and recycle simply everything, I asked James if he knew of an electrician who could come and have a look at it. It had also occurred to me that if we did not repair the set and threw it away, we would be accused of undermining the 'indigenous market for Indian goods' as explained by the inspector in the customs shed at the airport, if we could not produce the radiogram, when we left India at the end of the course.

Ranjit arrived on a bike, took a quick look and said that yes, he could fix the problem, but he would have to take it away and it would probably take a whole day. I was, to say the least, very pleasantly surprised that he was so confident and that he could do it so quickly. The transformer had about twelve different coloured wires attached to the various windings and there was no chance of me supplying a manual, so I wondered how he was going to achieve this. Even though you will see Indians loading the most amazing things onto a bicycle, I asked him how he was going to get this large and heavy radiogram onto his bike. He looked at me as though I had crawled out from under a stone, selected his best snips and cut the twelve wires, without so much as a record of the colour code or connection to the various amplifiers and lamps in the radiogram, pocketed the transformer and rode off on his bicycle.

The next day he returned, spent no more than five minutes with a soldering iron and went on his way. The radiogram is still working, installed in my workshop, twenty-seven years later.

Some Indian road signs and a crocodile warning

We teamed up with the Australian Brigadier on the NDC course and both families travelled to Kashmir just before the troubles became so severe that it was considered far too dangerous to visit this beautiful state. Two of the road signs just had to be photographed.

*Fellow NDC student, Australian Brigadier Frank Hickling and I are bemused by the Kashmiri road signs.
Frank was later Lt General and Chief of the Army.*

MY BAGS ARE IN THE BACK

My son, Justin, having trouble believing this road sign.

Much later on we came across a sign, which we considered just had to be someone winding us up – but then again! This was in a game reserve.

An (almost) unbelievable sign in a game reserve.

We nearly lost an Air Commodore

Throughout the course, various visits were arranged to different parts of the country, to neighbouring countries, to foreign countries further away and to the three armed services. Our visit to the Indian Navy involved a few days in Bombay, now renamed Mumbai, and after the formal visits to various ships and establishments we were given an afternoon off to enjoy as we wished. The Australian Brigadier on the course, Brigadier Frank Hickling[22], and I decided to accept the offer from the Navy to take a small 16ft dinghy for a sail around Bombay harbour. Having changed and rigged the dinghy, we were preparing to launch the boat when a fellow student, Air Commodore Manjit Singh, approached us and asked if he could join us. We were delighted to take him and asked if he had any sailing experience, in case he wanted to take the helm. It transpired that our Sikh friend had not only never set foot in a dinghy or sailing boat of any description, he couldn't swim either.

Manjit was suitably dressed in sensible civilian clothes, apart from his footwear, in the form of a pair of flip-flops and of course he was still sporting his turban. He donned a life jacket and we launched the dinghy and settled Manjit on the leeward side as we set off on a broad reach towards the centre of the vast harbour. The weather was perfect with a very reasonable breeze, which occasionally caused both Frank and I to sit 'out' to keep the boat on a reasonable keel. Whenever we keeled over and the leeward gunwale was almost or actually awash, Manjit would ask, in a slightly tremulous voice: "Should I come up there with you two?"

We reassured him that everything was under control and he should sit tight so we could control the trim. Everything went very smoothly as we crossed the harbour, passing a multitude of ships of different types, and Frank and I took turns on the helm. I can't recall who was on the helm as we approached a particularly large tanker and predictably lost some way as her bulk took our wind. Frank and I were sitting in when we emerged from the dead area and as we felt the wind freshen, moved to sit out again. At this, Manjit decided that

---

[22] Later promoted Lieutenant General as Chief of Army Staff, June 1998-July 2000.

the sight of both of us moving together was the prompt for him to move from his position close to the rushing water, up to the windward side. We told him to stay where he was but he was persistent and kept coming.

As he tried to step over the centreboard, being careful to keep low and not catch his turban on the close-hauled boom, he slipped and clattered back down to the gunwale, toppled and disappeared over the side with commendable style. The effect on the boat's trim was instantaneous as we both tried vainly to correct the sudden loss of Manjit. We were over in an instant.

Frank and I managed a reasonably dignified entry into the revoltingly dirty water of the harbour and checked for Manjit, but were horrified to see that the only sign of our friend was a pair of flip-flops and a turban, adrift a few feet from the hull. Manjit suddenly popped up, his life jacket fulfilling its purpose, and we breathed a sigh of relief, albeit with a big smile as we saw him turbanless for the first time ever.

As we got ourselves sorted out and prepared to right the boat, we were approached by a clinker-built motorboat with an impressive-looking Indian standing in the stern sheets, in flannels and a dark blue blazer and a large megaphone in one hand.

"Lower your mainsail before you try to bring her up!" he called across the water.

I glared at him and was about to reply when Frank, who outranked me, took control and suggested that the Indian megaphone-man could rearrange his travel plans and leave us to it, since we knew exactly what to do.

Megaphone-man appeared rather disenchanted that his assistance was being spurned and instructed his coxswain to turn away. At that moment we realised that he was supervising a nearby dinghy race, but were more concerned with our own immediate problems, one of which concerned the warning we had received about not drinking a single drop of Bombay harbour water. We did right the boat, bailed her out and decided to return to the naval base and call it a day.

That evening, the group of fifteen students from the National Defence College were invited to a reception hosted by the Royal Bombay Yacht Club and as one would expect, it was an exceptionally traditional event with a formal welcoming line at the entrance. As we got towards the front of the line a terrible thought crossed my mind and my fears were confirmed when the distinguished looking Commodore of the Club, welcoming his guests, stared inquisitively at me.

"Have we met before?" he asked.

"I don't think so Commodore," I replied. "This is my first trip to Bombay."

I left Frank and Manjit, in the line behind me to sort themselves out, but I did notice the Commodore staring at me occasionally throughout the evening with a quizzical and doubtful look on his face.

1989 - MOD, ORDNANCE BOARD

When I returned from India, having been awarded an MPhil (Unrecognised) from Allahabad University for my year's studies of International Relations, I moved on to my next appointment with hope and expectation, albeit with the realisation that I knew absolutely nothing about the Ordnance Board. Research revealed that it had been founded the year before Agincourt in 1415 and some wag told me just before I joined, that some of the founder members were still serving there.

The Board was situated in Empress State Building, once the tallest commercial building in London, overlooking the Earls Court Exhibition centres and West Brompton tube station. Current records state that it was built between 1958 and 1961, which must mean that when I attended my medical, before being accepted into the Navy, in this very building, it must have been in its first few months of usage.

The purpose of the Board was to ensure that all ordnance being introduced into service, whether for the Navy, Army or Air Force, was 'Safe and Suitable for Service'. My area of responsibility as a Member of the Board, covered Naval Guided Weapons and this meant that I was responsible for producing documentation known as Proceedings or 'Procs'. Unfortunately, in my nine months at the Board I failed, dismally, to produce a single Proc, which since these were seen to be a measure of productivity, did seem to indicate that I had 'could have done better'. I maintain, on the other hand, that since there were no new Naval Guided Weapons being introduced into service at that time, that there was very little for me to study, assess, critique and therefore I was constrained and unable to submit the appropriate Proc to the Board members for their agreement.

When I attended my last Board meeting, I was subjected to an embarrassing moment when the Board considered a Proc that noted the appointment of my successor and recorded my contribution in the following text.

Secretary informs the Board that Captain J A Aston, BSc, CEng, MIEE, RN has been appointed a Member of the Board with effect from 19 Dec 89, vice Captain (No Procs) Galloway, MSc, CEng, FIEE, RN, Belligerent of the Board and Beguiler of the Bench; Provoker of the President, Clamper of Vices, Mentor of Members and Sharpener of the Secretary; Sceptic of Standards, Tamperer of Traditions, Questioner of Qualifications and Reviser of Regulations; Steward of the Snooker Table and Bard of the Bar; Spinner of Fine Yarns and Chronicler of Ki; whose Type 23 Frigate turned out to be flat topped, armed with Sea Dart and to have embarked Harriers.

The Rear Admiral who signed this as President of the Board had summarised my Naval career theretofore, with amazing accuracy and I left feeling rather proud that my contribution had at least been noted, albeit I never did understand the last reference to the Type 23 Frigate.

1990 / 1992 - MOD, DIRECTORATE OF SCIENCE (SEA)

Within the Ministry of Defence, each of the three services had a directorate responsible for various scientific aspects required to support their everyday business and I joined as the Deputy Director of the Directorate of Science (Sea) and the only serviceman amongst a group of very talented scientists.

The unforgettable US Marine Colonel

One of many important subjects requiring scientific research and support for the Royal Navy was that of oceanography and particularly the effect of the ocean conditions on sonar performance. This oceanographic work consumed a fair part of my business week in London until one day I was chosen to attend American Naval War College (NWC) annual War Gaming event, in Newport, Rhode Island. The NWC educates and develops leaders, supports the defining of the future Navy and associated roles and missions, supports combat readiness and strengthens global maritime partnerships.

War Gaming involves groups of senior service and civilian personnel studying various political/military scenarios and, through an iterative process, developing war plans to guide the operations of the US Navy.

I found myself on 1st August 1990, sitting with some very

experienced and senior people from several 'friendly' countries and with a wide spectrum of backgrounds. There were about twelve of us around the table when we received our scenario, which envisaged the forces of Saddam Hussein invading Kuwait, and our task was to game the response from the US forces and their allies, both in the area and generally.

Across the table from me was a tough-looking US Marine Colonel who soon started to huff and puff about the scenario and when I started to remonstrate with him that it was not really our task to question the problem we had been set, he leant across the table and whispered, "There's no (blanked) way that that (blanked) idiot could invade (blanked) anything. He hasn't got the (blanked) troops, he hasn't got the (blanked) equipment and he certainly hasn't got the (blanked) brains to pull it off. We're wasting our (blanked) time here, Peter."

I couldn't persuade him that we had to go along with the wishes of the College faculty staff and get on with it, and at that point he set off on his own invasion plan, which involved the doughnut trolley. The next day, Saddam Hussein did invade Kuwait.

When we re-convened to assimilate this shattering news, the Colonel was sitting opposite me again. He beckoned to me, leant across and practically hoisted me in the air with an energetic grip on my uniform lapels and whispered, even more softly than yesterday, "If you mention to anyone, what I (blanked)-well said yesterday, I am going to come round there and (blanked)-well sort you out."

We became very good friends over the next two weeks.

Desert Storm

During the Desert Shield and Desert Storm phases of the Gulf War from August 1990 until February 1991, the British and the Americans wanted to collect, collate and make optimum use of various data that was being generated in the various actions in the Middle East. Agreement was reached that the two organisations in the UK and the USA with the responsibility for date collection should work together and share resources. I was tasked to lead the UK effort and set off for America. My American counterpart turned out to be much younger than me, female, extremely bright and extraordinarily beautiful.

Over the next few weeks and months we achieved what we had been tasked to do and we established an efficient and effective working relationship. At one stage when she visited UK with a couple of colleagues, I was told that when the Americans started to cast for the film Top Gun, the director, Tony Scott, spotted the young lady in question, then a young statistician at Miramar airbase and suggested that Maverick, a.k.a. Tom Cruise, needed some romantic involvement and so was created the role of the flight instructor Charlie Blackwood. I could well understand why they had cast Kelly McGillis in the role.

The American breakfast

During those two weeks in Rhode Island, we grew to enjoy the American attitude to service, especially in restaurants, where nothing was too much trouble, especially if they found out you were in the Navy. There was one favourite restaurant we frequented on several evenings, where an RN identity card ensured a 50% discount on a lobster dish and even my wife who accompanied me for the trip, at my expense of course, was entitled as well.

As an aside, but as another illustration of the American attitude to servicemen and women, I recall being told we were entitled to a discount on any rail fare, on production of an ID card. At the end of the War-gaming we wanted to travel to New York by train and accordingly produced the ID card at the ticket office. A charming girl looked quizzically at the RN card and asked, "Which navy is this then?"

When I explained that the Royal Navy was the British or UK navy, she broke into a broad grin and came back with, "Do you know Prince Charles then?"

When I mentioned that yes, I had met him and indeed her Majesty the Queen as well, I thought we were going to be upgraded. We did indeed get the discount.

Back to the subject of the way they carry the art of service in restaurants to a different level. I had got used, over the two weeks at the War College, to being asked to specify, in very precise detail, what I wanted, whether it was a simple cup of coffee, a piece of toast or a full-blown meal. So a request for coffee would be followed up with something like, "Do you want Americano, Breve, Latte, Mocha, Cappuccino, Espresso Lungo, Viennese Coffee?" and so on and so on.

On our last day at Rhode Island we decided to have breakfast at a splendid diner just outside the War College grounds. It was the archetypal American classic diner with a stainless steel exterior and as we entered, I turned to my wife.

"We just need a cop to ride up on his motorbike and we have a film set."

At this the policeman obliged and drove up. It was all far too much fun. Anyway, the plan was for me to order my breakfast in such a way that the waitress could definitely not come back to ask me to specify any detail whatsoever. Lynn ordered her breakfast and I took a big breath.

"Good morning. I would like two eggs easy over, on two slices of toasted rye bread, with a rasher of streaky bacon, grilled not fried, hash browns, one fried tomato, a field mushroom, fried, tomato catsup on the side, a small glass of freshly- squeezed orange juice and a large Americano black coffee, please."

I felt confident that I had achieved my aim, especially when the waitress beamed at my word-perfect delivery and the use of the word catsup. However, her response was not what I had wanted.

"Is that to eat in or take away, Sir?"

1993-95 - NAVAL ADVISER TO BRITISH HIGH COMMISSIONER, NEW DELHI

A dinner for eight Victoria Cross holders

Lynn and I had arrived in Delhi in early 1993 and one of the first and most enjoyable tasks was to coordinate the arrangements for the Victoria Cross holders who were about to fly to the UK for the 17th Reunion of the VC & GC Association on 27th May.

The Association started life as the VC Association on 27th June 1956, when 13 UK VCs and 11 Commonwealth VCs met in London. In 1962, at the 3rd Reunion of the VC Association, a decision was made to invite holders of the George Cross to full membership and as a result the association was renamed the "Victoria Cross & George Cross Association".

My role was to ensure that the eight VC holders in the Indian Sub-continent attending the Reunion, arrived in Delhi, had the necessary paperwork and caught the BA flight to London, together with one member of the family allowed to accompany them to the UK, normally a son or grandson. All went well as the VCs arrived in Delhi until it transpired that one VC had lost his passport. Hmm! You need to understand that the bureaucracy in India means that a passport application for an Indian National can take months. Two problems. The VC holder was Nepalese and I had twenty-four hours to obtain the passport and obtain a visa. No pressure then. We'll call the passport loser GG. See if you can spot him later.

It was a very hot day when we set off for the passport office. GG sat in my air-conditioned Land Rover while I, in very best uniform and full aiguillettes, approached the rugby scrum of some 400 applicants. The queuing system in India is an unbelievable experience, especially when it is about 42deg. Even if one does get to the front of a queue, there is no chance of being served since an Indian is somehow capable of wriggling between you and the counter and popping up with a big grin. I decided to play the diplomatic card and bypassed the queue, going straight to the office of the Chief Passport Officer. Striding with misplaced imperial importance I decided to adopt the Indian approach and barged through the throng of some twenty applicants seeking the final rubber stamp to authorize the issue of a passport. Even then as I placed the form on the top of the pile of forms, a hand appeared from behind me, slipped a form from the bottom of the pile and placed it on top of mine. Two hours and many slapped wrists later, we had GG's passport.

On the day before their departure, we invited the group of VCs with their accompanying family member to our "bungalow", a splendid two-storey, three-bedroom house within the BHC compound. We explained the flight arrangements, courtesy of BA who were upgrading the party from Economy to Club and the planned program of activities in London. After a while one of the VCs was feeling under the weather and we suggested a quiet lie down upstairs and asked our bearer, Shekhawat, to look in on him occasionally. An hour later it appeared that he had recovered somewhat as we saw Shekhawat slide past the sitting room door with a silver salver, bearing a pint of beer. A remarkable recovery.

Before the dinner that evening, GG took me aside to present me with a small kukri to thank me for the passport and of course it remains a very prized possession. The honour we felt having eight VCs in the house is difficult to express, but it was a truly outstanding evening.

*The eight Victoria Cross holders at Bungalow One for dinner.
L to R: Gaje Ghale, Umrao Singh, Bhandari Ram, Bhanbhagta Gurung, Gian
Singh, Agansingh Rai, Ganju Lama, and Rambahadur Limbu.
(Three British Airways staff behind)*

Apart from Rambahadur Limbu, gazetted in 1966 for action in Sarawak, the other seven VCs were born between 1919 and 1922 and gazetted for actions in 1943, 44 and 45.

We were further honoured when they all signed the visitors' book.

An amazing entry in our Visitors' Book.

The next day I accompanied the group to the airport, then a fairly shambolic setup and became agitated as these eminent people were made to queue for what seemed an unnecessarily long time as a clerk checked their paperwork and attacked a computer keyboard. I decided to intervene to speed up the process and went to enter the departure area and assist the clerk. I was stopped by a guard who looked at my diplomatic passport and asked me to "sign in". A dusty book appeared from beneath the counter. The last entry was dated 1947 and the headings on the columns were "prisoners' names", "guard" and so on. I signed in as James Bond and was accompanying Mary Poppins. The guard let me through and I approached the jobsworth clerk, still tapping away on his computer keyboard. When I pointed out that his terminal was not switched on and that he was wasting my time and his energy, things speeded up and the group went through in seconds.

I had arranged through the BA staff that a letter would be handed to the Captain of the aircraft explaining the background of the party and apparently this was announced to all passengers in the 747, when they were airborne, saying that anyone who wished to visit Club Class to shake hands and chat would be welcome. This resulted, I am told in a five-hour party in Club Class.

Time has moved on and I have read, over the years, of the deaths of many of these brave and utterly remarkable people. The entries in the gazette of their actions are amazing, are recommended reading and are summarized here:

Havildar (later Subadar) Gaje Ghale VC, 2nd Bn. 5th Royal Gurkha Rifles, Indian Army

During the period 24/27 May1943 in the Chin Hills, Burma. Havildar Gaje Ghale was in charge of a platoon of young soldiers engaged in attacking a strong Japanese position. Wounded in the arm, chest and leg, he nevertheless continued to lead assault after assault, encouraging his men by shouting the Gurkha's battle-cry. Spurred on by the irresistible will of their leader, the platoon stormed and captured the position which the Havildar then held and consolidated under heavy fire, refusing to go to the Regimental Aid post until ordered to do so.

Naik Gian Singh VC, 15th Punjab Regiment, Indian Army

On 2nd March 1945 on the road between Kamye and Myingyam, Burma, where the Japanese were strongly positioned, Naik Gian Singh, who was in charge of the leading section of his platoon, went on alone, firing his tommy gun, and rushed the enemy foxholes. In spite of being wounded in the arm, he went on, hurling grenades. He attacked and killed the crew of a cleverly concealed anti-tank gun and then led his men down a lane clearing all enemy positions. He went on leading his section until the action had been satisfactorily completed.

Rifleman (later Lance-Naik) Bhanbhagta Gurung VC, 3rd Bn. 2nd Gurkha Rifles, Indian Army

On 5th March 1945 at Snowdon East, near Tamandu, Burma, a section was pinned down by heavy enemy fire and was also being subjected to sniping from a tree. Rifleman Bhanbhagta Gurung killed the sniper and later when the section was again attacked, he dashed forward under continuous fire personally clearing four enemy foxholes and he also silenced a light machine-gun. With the help of a Bren gunner and two riflemen he then repelled an enemy counter-attack on the captured bunker with heavy losses. His action in clearing these positions was decisive in capturing the objective.

Naik (later Havildar) Agansing Rai VC, MM, 2nd Bn., 5th Gurkha Rifles, Indian Army

On 26th June 1944 at Bishenpur, Burma, Naik Agansing Rai led his section in an attack on one of two posts, which had been taken by the enemy and were now threatening our communications. Under withering fire the Naik and his party charged a machine gun, he himself killing three of the crew. The first position having been taken, he then led a dash on a machine-gun firing from the jungle, where he killed three of the crew, his men accounting for the rest. He subsequently tackled an isolated bunker single-handed, killing all four occupants. The enemy were now so demoralized that they fled and the second post was captured.

Rifleman (later Subadar) Ganju Lama VC, MM 1st Bn. 7th Gurkha Rifles, Indian Army

On 12th June 1944 at Ninthoukhong, Burma, B Company was attempting to stem the enemy's advance when it came under heavy machine-gun and tank machine-gun fire. Rifleman Ganju Lama with complete disregard for his own safety, took his Piat gun and crawling forward, succeeded in bringing the gun into action within 30 yards of the enemy tanks, knocking out two of them. Despite a broken wrist and two other serious wounds to his right and left hands he then moved forward and engaged the tank crew who were trying to escape. Not until he had accounted for all of them did he consent to have his wounds dressed.

Sepoy (later Subadar) Bhandari Ram VC, 10th Baluch Regiment, Indian Army

On 22nd November 1944 at East Mayu, Burma, Sepoy Bhandari Ram's platoon was pinned down by machine-gun fire. Although wounded, he crawled up to a Japanese light machine-gun in full view of the enemy and was wounded again, but continued crawling to within 5 yards of his objective. He then threw a grenade into the position, killing the gunner and two others. This action inspired his platoon to rush and capture the enemy position. Only then did he allow his wounds to be dressed.

Lance-Corporal (later Captain) Rambahadur Limbu VC MVO 2nd Bn., Princess Mary's Gurkha Rifles

On 21st Nov 1965 in Sarawak, Lance-corporal Rambahadur Limbu was in an advance party of 16 Gurkhas when they encountered about 30 Indonesians holding a position on the top of a jungle-covered hill. The Lance Corporal went forward with two men, but when they were only 10 yards from the machine-gun, the sentry opened fire, whereupon the NCO rushed forward and killed him with a grenade. The enemy then opened fire on the small party wounding the two men with the Lance Corporal who, under heavy fire, made two journeys into the open to drag his comrades to safety.

Havildar (later Subadar-Major) Umrao Singh VC, Royal Indian Artillery

On 15/16th Dec 1944 in the Kaladan Valley, Burma, Havildar Umrao Singh, who was in charge of a gun in an advanced section of his battery, repeatedly beat off enemy attacks. In the final assault on the objective he struck down three of the enemy in hand-to-hand fighting and later, when found exhausted and wounded beside his gun there were ten of the enemy lying dead around him. The gun was still in working order and was in action again that day.

White-water rafting on the Ganges

It was a bit of a custom for staff from the High Commission to have a few days break at Easter and travel for several hours by car, one hundred and fifty miles to the North-North-East to a beach on the river Ganges, to the north of Rishikesh. A 'beach' on the Ganges does sound bizarre, but in fact the river does indeed have the most beautifully white areas of sand adjoining the river and these are vast.

Our campsite on the Ganges, just a few miles from the Chinese border.

Camp was set up and we enjoyed first class safari-style accommodation in tents pitched on the beach, with a large dining area, beneath the canopy of a time-expired parachute. The beach is pure white and very squeaky as you walk and composed of deposits from the glaciers not that far distant.

After breakfast we would be driven to the start-point for the day's rafting and then, donning the appropriate gear, board our rafts, which are of course massively strong rubber inflatables of different sizes, capable, in our case, of taking ten plus a coxswain. Some of the rapids were merely ripples, which scarcely merited attention but others were more daunting and some were downright dangerous, including one which had, in times past, claimed lives by virtue of a whirlpool.

Typical small rapid.

We were also allowed to 'body-surf' through certain sections of the rapids, where the incredibly cold water was deep enough and the water totally docile. As long as one wore a life jacket and protective helmet, lay on one's back with feet downriver, there was no risk to life or limb.

One morning we were woken by the distinctive sound of timber being chopped and when we emerged from the tent, saw several figures on the other bank of the Ganges, building a pyre. They had managed to climb down a very steep one hundred foot cliff with a shrouded body between them and were clearly about to cremate the body before committing the remains to the sacred river. Unfortunately there was not much in the way of wood on the riverbank that they had chosen and the pyre was a miserable affair. When they set fire to the pyre, the flames were equally unimpressive and when they rolled the shroud into the river, one was definitely left with the impression that not much had been achieved on the pyre. Needless to say, some bright spark cheered everyone up during breakfast by suggesting that it was quite conceivable that we might catch the body up that morning, so bodysurfing might be problematical.

We set off, that morning from the campsite itself and so our thoughts were definitely focussed on the funeral we had witnessed and the passage of the body down the very waters we were now rafting. It wasn't long before our guide said that the next rapids were perfect for bodysurfing and whilst some declined the opportunity, most of us got prepared. The High Commissioner, Sir Nicholas, and his wife, Lady Sue, were quickly into the water, as was I, together with about four more from our raft. I have to admit that I made sure I drifted towards one of the other wives and when close enough, mentioned that I am sure I had felt something bump into my leg a few seconds ago, at which I gently tapped her on her calf. The scream was impressive.

A few minutes later in a particularly strong eddy I found myself virtually entangled with Lady Sue, with arms and legs in all sorts of incorrect places, at which we both mumbled an apology and a bit of a silly giggle which Sir Nicholas, a few yards downstream clearly heard.

"Are you alright darling?" he called back over his shoulder.

"I'm fine," replied Lady Sue, "I'm in the hands of the Naval Adviser."

"That's what I'm worried about," retorted Sir Nicholas.

The SAS come to stay for a month

Unfortunately, during our tour in India, there was a kidnapping in Kashmir involving back-packers from four different countries, including the UK. Each country despatched Special Forces personnel to New Delhi to assist in determining their location and possible release. Two SAS personnel arrived and since we had a large bungalow, known as Bungalow One, which was in fact a large three-bedroom house, within the High Commission compound, it was decided that they would stay with us for the duration of their mission.

Bungalow One, British High Commission.

They arrived with a vast amount of electronic equipment and I decided to vacate the study and hand it over for their operations centre. They spent a while setting up the equipment, much of which was American, and I waited for signs of activity to indicate communication with whoever, had been established. Nothing happened until the SAS officer appeared and asked, in a rather meek manner, if I had a UK to USA telephone adapter.

A few days later, it was clear that the location of the kidnappers and their victims had been established and it was decided that we would try to get some provisions to them, as a sign of goodwill, but more importantly so that we could include a beacon in the package which could track their future movements, should they decamp. The SAS duo asked if they could place a cardboard box, containing several cartons of long-life milk, as well as the beacon in the middle of our lawn for an hour, while the satellite passed overhead to establish proper operation.

Bungalow One garden.

At that time, there was the very slightest chance of a monsoon rain shower and the SAS asked if we could arrange for someone to look after the device and be ready to protect it with an umbrella if needed. The Mali,[23] Ram, who incidentally spoke not a word of English, was instructed to loiter in the shade of a tree at the edge of the lawn, watch for the first sign of rain and then rush out with the

---
[23] The gardener.

umbrella to protect the cardboard box. Our bearer explained all of this and stressed that his future career as our Mali depended on his performance in protecting the carton.

The hour passed, as did the satellite, and we were told that Hereford were content with the beacon's performance and that it should be deployed as soon as possible. As the SAS team picked the box up, one of them suggested that it looked a little bit too clean and could do with a bit of distressing.

"What do you suggest?" I asked.

"Do you think Ram could get us a bit of dirt and a watering can?" came the reply.

When Ram had provided the necessary, the Sergeant upended the watering can over the box, sprayed it generously and then proceeded to rub soil into the wet cardboard.

I often wonder if Ram is sitting at home in Delhi, right now, telling his grandchildren about the way the British leave a box in the middle of a lawn for an hour, making sure it can not possibly get wet and then, when the hour has passed, pour water over it and rub in some soil.

Lynn's driving skills in Delhi

One Sunday, when matters were relatively quiet for the SAS duo, Lynn told them that she was going to 'The Fence', a popular spot in Delhi for casual clothing and they were welcome to join her, if they wished. They jumped at the chance.

We had a new Land Rover Discovery and Lynn had readily mastered driving in Delhi and drove fast, fearlessly and with exceptional skill and indeed enjoyment. However, to the un-initiated, a short drive through the chaos of Delhi traffic was a total nightmare.

Typical scene with lorry broken down on the left as indicated by the tiny rock in the middle of the road (about a yard behind the driver – not the clearly visible jack under the axle), while the slightly overloaded lorry squeezes past.

Lynn suggested that the SAS duo might like to read a recent article in the Times of India which neatly summarised the driving experience in India and which would prepare them for what they were to witness.

Travelling in India is an almost hallucinatory potion of sound, spectacle and experience. It is frequently heart-rending, sometimes hilarious, mostly exhilarating, always unforgettable ---- and, when you are on the roads, extremely dangerous.

To the Westerner, the behaviour of drivers seems to cross Space Invaders with a profound belief in reincarnation. The Ambassador cars, Bombay derivatives of the Fifties Morris Oxford, rattle tourists to palaces and temples like time capsules in a game of virtual unreality. There is an explanation for this behaviour. Most Indian road users observe a version of the Highway Code based on a Sanskrit text. These twelve rules of the Indian road are published for the first time in English.

ARTICLE I: The assumption of immortality is required for all road users

ARTICLE II: Indian traffic, like Indian society, is structured on a strict caste system. The following precedence must be accorded at all times. In descending order, give way to: cows, elephants, heavy trucks, buses, official cars, camels, light trucks, buffalo, jeeps, ox-carts, private cars, motorcycles, scooters, auto-rickshaws, pigs, pedal rickshaws, goats, bicycles (passenger carrying), dogs, pedestrians.

ARTICLE III: All wheeled vehicles shall be driven in accordance with the maxim: To slow is to falter, to brake is to fail, to stop is defeat. This is the Indian driver's mantra.

ARTICLE IV: Use of horn (also known as the sonic fender or aural amulet):

Cars (IV, 1, a-c): Short blasts (urgent) indicate supremacy, i.e. in clearing dogs, rickshaws and pedestrians from path. Long blasts (desperate) denote supplication, i.e. to oncoming truck, "I am going too fast to stop, so unless you slow down we shall both die." In extreme cases, this may be accompanied by flashing of headlights (frantic). Single blast (casual) means "I have seen someone out of India's population of 870 million[24] whom I recognise"; "There is a bird in the road (which at this speed could go through my windscreen)", or "I have not blown my horn for several minutes."

Trucks and buses (IV, 2, a): All horn signals have the same meaning, viz, "I have an all-up weight of approximately 12½ tons and have no intention of stopping, even if I could." This signal may be emphasised by the use of headlamps (insouciant).

Article IV: remains subject to the provision of Order of Precedence in Article II above.

ARTICLE V: All manoeuvres, use of horn and evasive action shall be left until the last possible moment.

ARTICLE VI: In the absence of seat belts (which there is), car occupants shall wear garlands of marigolds. These should be kept fastened at all times.

---

[24] 1995 population figure.

ARTICLE VII: Rights of Way: Traffic entering a road from the left has priority. So does traffic from the right, and also traffic in the middle. Lane discipline (VII, I); All Indian traffic at all times and irrespective of direction of travel shall occupy the centre of the road.

ARTICLE VIII: Roundabouts: India has no roundabouts. Apparent traffic islands in the middle of crossroads have no traffic management function. Any other impression should be ignored.

ARTICLE IX: Overtaking is mandatory. Every moving vehicle is required to overtake every other moving vehicle, irrespective of whether it has just overtaken you. Overtaking should only be undertaken in suitable locations, such as in the face of oncoming traffic, on blind bends, at junctions and in the middle of villages/city centres. No more than two inches should be allowed between your vehicle and the one you are passing --- one inch in the case of bicycles or pedestrians.

ARTICLE X: Nirvana may be obtained through the head-on crash.

ARTICLE XI: Reversing: No longer applicable since no vehicle in India has reverse gear.

ARTICLE XII: The 10th incarnation of God was as an articulated tanker.

Finally, because she wasn't sure they understood what was to befall them, she showed them the High Commission copy of the "Frequently Asked Questions" and staff answers, for newly arrived members of staff wishing to drive in Delhi.

How do I turn into a road?

When you approach a road and know you are going to turn into it across the oncoming traffic, start the approach as far back as possible and disrupt as many cars as you possibly can. Remember to blow your horn and flash your lights.

Do I ever slow down?

Yes, you either stop or go very slowly when someone is having a fight or when there is an accident. You may stop as long as you wish. It may cause a blockage and the horns will be very troublesome but, if you are interested in the consequences of the outcome, by all means stay as long as you wish. Just ignore the horns --- other drivers can become rather impatient at times like this. It is important to remember that you are interested and nothing else matters.

Can I carry a pillion passenger on my motorbike?

You can carry as many as you wish, four being a convenient number. You, as the driver, are the only one who must wear a helmet. It can be any sort of helmet. Construction helmets come in may colours, so look better, are probably cheaper, and do not clutter up the face so much. Remember that your wife must ride sidesaddle, with the baby in her arms. During the monsoon, she can carry both baby and umbrella. Your young children find riding on the petrol tank comfortable.

Am I safe riding a bike?

No. A bicycle is the smallest vehicle on the road, so it is the lowest in the pecking order. A bus or truck is best and you can be Lord of the road. They have very loud horns.

Are there rules at roundabouts?

Most of the time you go clockwise. Sometimes you go anti-clockwise. When on the roundabout, you must stop to let incoming traffic from the side roads go in front of you. Yes, it is disruptive and it fouls up the roundabout. Where there is a roundabout, there is usually also a policeman, sometimes two, and traffic lights. It seems usual to take notice of one of the policemen and disregard the lights and the roundabout. The policemen often ignore them and this is when you go anti-clockwise. Remember that nothing is a surprise. If there are no policemen on duty, you just do what you like anyway and ignore all the signals.

What happens if I have an accident?

It pays to abscond immediately after an accident. It is noted in the 'The News' that after a bus accident, the driver absconds - so, when in Rome...

Are there any rules for pedestrians?

On no account look right or left before crossing the road. Try not to use the footpaths too often, as you will interfere with the bikes and motorbikes.

What do the road markings mean?

No one is quite sure what they mean, but the general opinion is that they are there to show you there is a road underneath.

Are rickshaws safe to ride in?

Their function is to prove to you that a camel can pass through the eye of a needle. It can be a very scary experience to ride in one. If you want to try it, just imagine that you are at the fairground and have paid to do this for fun.

What do I do if my vehicle breaks down?

On no account move your vehicle from where it has stopped. It does not matter where it is on the road. You must collect rocks and surround the entire vehicle with a ring of them so that everyone else knows that it has broken down. After your vehicle has been fixed, just drive away and leave the ring of rocks. This in turn ensures that there will soon be another breakdown in exactly the same place and rocks will be easy to find.

Are there any special rules when I ride my motorbike?

Yes, there are. You ignore all of the above and do whatever you like.

Why do policemen blow their whistles?

If you find out, please advise the Management Section as soon as possible.

I was at home when the trio returned from the shopping expedition and noticed that the SAS Officer looked rather pale and drawn as he passed through the hall and as the Sergeant followed, he caught my eye.

"She's b....y mad, your wife, you know Sir."

So much for the defensive training course at Hereford, I thought.

The striped croquet lawn

We were very lucky in Bungalow One, to have a large lawn at the rear of the property, which was ideal for entertaining but also doubled as an excellent croquet lawn. I was a little bit obsessed about the lawnmower being used to the best effect to leave really straight alternate dark and light stripes. However, trying to explain this to my Hindi-speaking gardener, Ram, through the good offices of my Urdu-speaking bearer, Shekhawat proved more than a challenge. It soon became obvious that a demonstration was required. Just before I set off to my office in the High Commission, 200 metres away, I asked Ram to get the lawnmower out. I then did four trips up and down the lawn, creating four alternate dark and light stripes. Ram was dumbstruck as to the pleasant effect created and I left for the office, confident that the croquet lawn was about to be transformed.

After work, I returned to find my wife Lynn grinning from ear to ear and eventually starting to giggle as I walked through the house to inspect the lawn. From a distance the stripes were surprisingly effective and the Mali had certainly got the alternate dark and light effect. However the cause for Lynn's amusement soon became apparent as I walked onto the veranda. Ram had apparently misunderstood the technique or perhaps forgotten the process, demonstrated so effectively by Sahib.

Lynn told me that he had mown one strip going away from the house, then walked the entire circumference of the lawn until he was back near the house again and mown the next strip, in the same direction as the first, but a suitable mower's width away. The tufted and striped effect was so impressive that we actually kept it for a few days, but of course croquet was a non-starter.

This was not the only 'misunderstanding' involving Ram and I was to learn a very valuable lesson on the next occasion that I tried to get a message of some importance to him.

The cocktail party with a distinctive aroma

We were about to host a large evening reception in the garden for senior Indian Service personnel, Commonwealth Advisers and foreign Attachés and it was essential that the house and garden looked at their best. Shekhawat, the bearer, and Alum, the cook, had everything in hand and employed additional staff as required. On the day of the reception, Ram, the Mali was instructed to mow the lawn and generally tidy up the shrubs and trees and pick flowers for the various arrangements.

I had noticed that Ram had, quite correctly, acquired a large mound of manure for fertilising the vegetable garden and the lawn at a later date and I was worried that the aroma emanating from this mighty pile could drift from the side of the house, so I got Shekhawat to tell Ram to cover it with an enormous sheet of polythene. I then committed the cardinal sin of confusing the issue by providing Ram with too much information.

"Whatever he does," I said to Shekhawat, "make sure he does not spread the manure on the lawn until after the reception. OK? No manure on the lawn."

"Koi baat nahi," [25] replied Shekhawat, and I went off to work feeling that that was another disaster avoided.

At about 1230, Lynn phoned to say she had just returned from the shops to find the whole lawn covered in brown, evil-smelling manure and that we might as well cancel the whole reception. The smell was unbelievable and there was no way it could be watered in or the smell eradicated. Tempers were running high and it was time to return to the house and find out why the Mali had been so determined to wreck this important event.

Shekhawat was summoned and Ram fallen in for Captain's defaulters.

"Please ask Ram why he has spread the manure all over the entire lawn, when I specifically told him not to do just that, until after the reception," I thundered.

---

[25] "No problem"

Shekhawat translated and we awaited a response from Ram, who, at this stage, appeared surprisingly relaxed.

"He says," replied Shekhawat, "that he did exactly what you suggested."

"But I told him 'No manure on lawn', so which part of that didn't he understand?" I spluttered.

"Ah," said Shekhawat with a smile, "Mali only understands the last three words of a sentence."

So there it was. It was all my mistake. Too much information. I should have said, "No manure today."

We moved the reception to a pleasant and remote garden area near the Moghul pool, a couple of hundred metres away in the High Commission grounds.

The Delhi Driving Test

The Indian government suddenly decided in 1994 that all diplomats should take an Indian driving test. Until then, we had all been granted immunity from such a test and this new procedure caused all sorts of concerns within the various Embassies and High Commissions. 'What sort of test was involved and what did we need to do to prepare?' were the questions echoing around the corridors and we were given no clue as to what was in store.

The British High Commission staff were allotted a particular day at the New Delhi test centre and told to present ourselves, en masse, at 1000 on the day. We arrived and were asked to form an orderly queue, an unprecedented event in India, and wait to be summoned to the inspector's office, behind the door ahead of us.

The door opened at 1000 exactly and the first Briton was called forward. A matter of 30 seconds later, the next candidate was summoned, but there was no sign of the first Briton. Perhaps he was doing the practical part of the test around the streets of Delhi, we pondered. I was called after a few minutes and found myself facing the inspector seated behind an imposing desk, the top of which was covered in a large sheet of Perspex, beneath which I saw a very large sheet of the international road signs.

The inspector pointed to one, the sign for a level crossing, and asked me what it was. Next came the 'Stop' sign. Both answers were clearly correct as he ended the procedure with a terse, "You've passed."

I was then invited to leave by a different door and found myself at the back of the main assembly area, behind the queue waiting to be 'tested'. Since we had shared vehicles to get to the test centre, I then waited for the rest of my group, which included the British nurse from our medical centre in the High Commission. She joined us a few minutes later, but was clearly distressed.

"What's the problem?" we all asked.

"I failed," she lamented. "What do I do now?"

At this, the Indian member of the locally employed staff at the High Commission, Dinesh Kumar, stepped up.

"Don't worry, memsahib. Just get back in the queue and do it again. He won't recognise you," he said with a big grin.

And that is how she passed her Indian driving test.

The Defence Services Staff College - Quetta to Wellington

One of my areas of responsibility concerned the general welfare of the British students at the Indian Defence Services Staff College (DSSC) at Wellington, in the state of Tamil Nadu, some 2,500 km south of my office in New Delhi. The one-year Staff Course included three UK students from any of the three services and before they started the course, I would meet the students and their families in Delhi and brief them on various aspects of the course and what lay in store for them in the year ahead. I would also try to visit them once during the year if possible and would always be available to resolve any particularly difficult problems, should they arise. This did indeed unfortunately arise for the wife of one student, when she broke her ankle in a riding incident and after surgery and various complications, she had to be moved to the our house in Delhi for further treatment in a specialist hospital and ultimately re-patriated to UK for further surgery.

Wellington is located in the Nilgiris[26] District of Tamil Nadu, approximately 80 km from Coimbatore and 14 km from the famous hill resort of Udhagamandalam (also called Ooty or Ootacamund). Wellington lies at an altitude of 1880 meters above mean sea level, and is blessed with a mild and salubrious climate throughout the year. The annual temperature varies from 3° C to 30° C.

The origins of the DSSC lie way back in time and it is worth digressing to understand why the College was established here, in southern India. It was in 1856 in England, that the British first felt the need for specially trained officers to improve their military efficiency. The Duke of Cambridge, then Commander-in-Chief, set the qualifications required of a staff officer and soon the senior department of the Royal Military College (established in 1802) at Sandhurst, was designated to train British officers in organizational skills and intellect, with a new name 'The Staff College'. The senior

---

[26] The word derives from the Hindi words Nila (blue) and Giris (mountains), and is said to be the name given to the hills when the British planted thousands of Eucalyptus trees to protect the tea plantations. Hence the well-known Nilgiri tea.

department began admitting students based on an examination. It had its own Commandant and professors and was open to officers of all arms. The first batch consisted of 30 students.

In 1862, the College shifted to Camberley and since 1864, officers who passed out of the College were distinguished by the letters 'psc' (passed staff course). The tradition continues 'till this day. The syllabus included mathematics, military history, topography, astronomy, French, German and Hindustani. The general officers in the field army required staff officers who could sketch rapidly, build bridges, make roads, construct field works, all very quickly and to be fluent linguists.

The Indian mutiny of 1857 came as a rude shock to the British. Subsequently, major reforms were constituted and the Indian Army was reorganized and reduced in strength. In 1868, under the Secretary of State for War, Edward Cardwell, a Royal Commission considered the possibility of a Staff College in India. Though an Indian Staff Corps had been set up to provide the Indian Army with British officers, they were not staff trained. General (later FM) Lord Strathnairn contended that India should have a Staff College of its own. However, the proposal was turned down. The Government felt that suitable instructors might not be available in India. Moreover, India presented an unsuitable climate and lack of opportunities to study modern battles.

Repeated requests were turned down until 1902, when Lord Kitchener took over as Commander-in-Chief. He proposed to establish an Indian Staff College, very similar to the one at Camberley, with the same regulations, syllabus, entrance examination, and a possible interchange of instructional staff, and also an inspection by the Camberley Commandant. Though his proposal met with the same apprehension, his efforts bore fruit and he was successful in overcoming all opposition. The proposal was sanctioned in 1905. An Indian Staff College was to be established in Quetta (now in Pakistan).

The first entrance exam was held on 15 May 1905 and the first course of two years' duration commenced on the 1st of July the same year. The first Commandant was Brig Gen AWL Bayly, CB, DSO, a Camberley graduate. In 1907, the College moved to Quetta and was officially opened on 1st of June, the same year, by Maj Gen (later Lt

Gen) HL Smith-Dorrien, who was then commanding the 4th (Quetta) Division. The aim of the College was to produce officers who could organise all the necessary staff arrangements that spell success in war.

The Staff College, Quetta, maintained close liaison with Camberley and even adopted the Owl with the motto "Tam Marte Quam Minerva" [27] as its own. The College closed down after the outbreak of the First World War, and the accommodation was transformed into a Cadet College to train young men for commission into the British and Indian armies. It was only in 1919 that the College started functioning again.

Quetta had its share of brilliant students and instructors. Field Marshal Slim attended the two-year course in 1926. Field Marshals Auchinleck and Montgomery were Chief Instructors between 1932 and 1937, in the rank of Colonel. The first King's Commissioned Indian Officer (KCIO) to attend the 1933-34 Staff Course was Captain KM Cariappa, later the first Indian Commander-in-Chief and Field Marshal.

The Staff College continued to operate throughout the Second World War but the matter of independence for India was high on the political agenda and in 1946 the UK despatched a Cabinet Mission to India to discuss and plan for the transfer of power from the British Government to Indian leadership. Formulated at the initiative of Clement Attlee, the Prime Minister, the mission consisted of Lord Pethick-Lawrence, the Secretary of State for India, Sir Stafford Cripps, President of the Board of Trade, and A. V. Alexander, the First Lord of the Admiralty. Lord Wavell, the Viceroy of India, did not participate.

The Cabinet Mission's purpose was threefold:

* Hold preparatory discussions with elected representatives of British India and the Indian states in order to secure agreement as to the method of framing the constitution.

* Set up a constitution body.

* Set up an Executive Council with the support of the main Indian parties.

---

[27] As much by skill as war.

MY BAGS ARE IN THE BACK

The Cabinet Mission arrived in India on 23 March 1946 and in Delhi on 2 April 1946.

The Mission held talks with the representatives of the Indian National Congress and the All-India Muslim League, the two largest political parties in the Constituent Assembly of India. The two parties planned to determine a power-sharing arrangement between Hindus and Muslims to prevent a communal dispute, and to determine whether British India would be better off unified or divided. The Congress party under Gandhi-Nehru nexus wanted to obtain a strong central government with more powers compared to state governments. The All India Muslim League under Jinnah, wanted to keep India united but with political safeguards provided to Muslims such as 'guarantee' of 'parity' in the legislatures. This stance of the League was backed up by the wide belief of Muslims that the British Raj was simply going to be turned into a 'Hindu Raj' once the British departed; and since the Muslim League regarded itself as the sole spokesman party of Indian Muslims, it was incumbent up on it to take the matter up with the Crown. After initial dialogue, the Mission proposed its plan over the composition of the new government on 16 May 1946. Agreement between the Congress and the Muslim League proved impossible.

Reaching an impasse, the British proposed a second, alternative plan on 16 June 1946. This plan sought to arrange for India to be divided into Hindu-majority India and a Muslim-majority India that would later be renamed Pakistan, since Congress had vehemently rejected 'parity' at the Centre. A list of princely states of India that would be permitted to accede to either dominion or attain independence was also drawn up.

The Viceroy began organizing the transfer of power to a Congress-League coalition. But League president Muhammad Ali Jinnah denounced the hesitant and conditional approval of the Congress and rescinded League approval of both plans.

Jinnah and the League condemned the new government, and vowed to agitate for Pakistan by any means possible. Disorder arose in Punjab and Bengal, including the cities of Delhi, Bombay and Calcutta. On the League-organized Direct Action Day, over 5,000 people were killed across India, and Hindu, Sikh and Muslim mobs began clashing routinely.

At the arrival of the new Viceroy, Lord Mountbatten of Burma on 24th March 1947, Congress leaders expressed the view that the coalition was unworkable and on 3rd June it was announced that the sub-continent would be divided on 15 August the same year.

Until this point the Defence Services had kept out of the controversy and went about their job as usual, but at this point Indian officers and men were offered the choice of service in the Armed Forces of either of the two Dominions or to serve neither. British officers were also given a similar choice. The Service headquarters and training establishments were split.

Colonel SD Verma[28], Indian Army, had been posted to Staff College, Quetta, in early 1947 to instruct a Division of 60 officers. On 'Partition,' a mixed Indian-Pakistani-British board was assembled to divide the assets of the College in the ratio of two to India and one to Pakistan. Colonel Verma and Major Zaheer represented Indian and Pakistani interests respectively. The Quetta library stayed with Pakistan and India got the Defence library located at Delhi. Other items included mess property, crockery, cutlery, cups, silver trophies and oil paintings. The division of the other assets posed little problem and the process was completed quite smoothly, except for one item.

There was a dispute about one particular piece of silver, the Camberley Owl, presented by General Sir H Rawlinson, Commandant at Camberley, when he visited the Staff College, Quetta in 1906. The inscription on the trophy stated quite clearly that it was 'Presented by the Staff College, Camberley, to the Indian Staff College'. Since the Staff College Quetta was no longer to be the Indian Staff College, the Trophy was eventually assigned to India and now adorns the Officers' Mess of Staff College, Wellington.

The Indian Army HQ chose to entrust the setting up of an Indian Staff College to Colonel Verma, and in early October 1947, he was sent a signal from the Director of Military Training, stating that he must proceed, reconnoitre and locate the new college, that should start functioning from the 1st of April 1948. The signal also stated that he had been appointed as the Commandant of Staff College, India.

---

[28] Later, Lieutenant General.

The Camberley Owl.

The 15th Staff Course at Quetta terminated on 10th of October 1947, with thirty-two Indian officer graduates. A special train, well escorted by some Baluch and Gorkha Jawans, left Quetta on 15th October 1947. Its passengers, the Indian officers, their families and many civilians reached Ambala Cantonment safely three days later.

Expecting more instructions, Colonel Verma reached Delhi to find everybody preoccupied with the mayhem in Kashmir. In Colonel Verma's, own words, "Eventually I managed to corner an officer in the Quartering Directorate and asked him to give me a list of places where there was some accommodation lying vacant. He was kind enough to give me a list, and then, as an afterthought, he said, 'Oh, yes and there are a few barracks and some empty British Other Ranks family quarters in a place called Wellington near Madras'."

After rejecting a variety of locations, Wellington stood out as a natural choice, with the exquisite Nilgiri hills as a picturesque backdrop, an ideal climate for the army man from Quetta, the decision was easily made. Additionally, the hills were ideal for mountain warfare exercises, the Coimbatore plains for mobile warfare and the Mysore jungles were reasonably easy to reach. On 3rd November 1947, Colonel Verma took a final decision and requested that the special train, with the Indian officers, their families and many civilians from Quetta be routed from Ambala in Haryana, 2,700 km south to Mettupalaiyam in Tamil Nadu and thence by metre gauge hill train up to Wellington.

After that not-so-brief, but hopefully interesting history lesson on the origins of the DSSC, let us return to the year 1993 when I was to accompany the High Commissioner, Sir Nicholas Fenn, on a visit to the College, where he was due to give a one hour lecture to the students. We checked in to a small but comfortable hotel in Coonor, 3kms from the DSSC, and all was well until later that evening he called me to his room to say that he was suffering from the most ghastly throat and had practically lost his voice, had a terrible temperature and felt awful. I immediately considered that we would have to cancel his lecture and said so, but was immediately corrected by a croaked, "You'll have to do it for me, Peter."

Sir Nicholas was an exceptional orator and there was no possible way that I could replicate his style of delivery, his experience or his knowledge especially when it came to the questions at the conclusion of his lecture, not to mention that I did not even know what the subject matter was.

"Could I have a copy of your lecture then, Sir?" I asked. "So I can start rehearsing and researching the subject."

The High Commissioner looked at me with a mixture of compassion, sorrow and pity and uttered the words I really did not want to hear.

"I don't actually use notes for my talks."

This is getting serious I thought and just hoped the subject matter was within my area of expertise.

"So what is the actual title of the talk, High Commissioner?"

Another painful look crossed his face as he pronounced, "The Indo-British relationship since Independence and the way ahead for optimising synergy between the two governments."

Brilliant, I thought. Absolutely brilliant. Almost the same subject I had been studying, like him, for the last few years.

I returned to my room to contemplate and consider whether I had time to develop the same ailment as the High Commissioner before the night was out. I didn't sleep much that night and after breakfast, went to call on Sir Nicholas's room suffering from something between trepidation and total panic. I was mightily relieved when my knock was answered by a reasonably lusty 'come in' and even more surprised by the total recovery he seemed to have engineered overnight. He was in good, if not perfect health, and ready to go. Relief would not describe the sensation I experienced. The lecture he delivered later that morning was riveting and the question and answer session, superb.

A Visit to Ootacamund (Ooty) and the rules of Snooker

After the DSSC visit, we drove a few kilometres to Ootacamund, (aka Ooty or Snooty Ooty), a beautiful town and its stunning beauty and splendid green deep valleys inspired the British to name it Queen of Hill Stations.

Ootacamund was discovered by the British around 1819, and they flocked there, and as their numbers grew, so did the need for a common meeting ground, and thus the Ootacamund Club came into being in October 1841.

The "Ooty" Club.

As membership increased over the years and with it the necessity of additional facilities, additions & alterations included a line of bedrooms being added in 1863, new chambers in 1898, & in 1904 a ladies' annex was constructed. In 1890, His Highness, the Maharaja of Vizianagaram presented a squash racquet court.

Stepping into the Club today, one is transported back in time and one is enveloped in panelled walls, parquet flooring, highly polished rosewood furniture & gleaming brass fittings. Circling the walls of the Mixed Bar are lists of past Masters of the Ootacamund Hunt from 1845 onwards, and also lists of winners of the Ladies Point to Point races, and of the Peter Pan Cup – presented to the Ootacamund Hunt by the planters of South India. The Ooty club is fondly referred to as the "Snooty Ooty Club" and also "The Morgue" , thanks to its many hunting trophies.

In 1983 I recall seeing pictures of Winston Churchill, amongst others, scattered throughout the club and particularly recall a mass of tables laid out for bridge with extending ledges to hold one's drink and it felt, incorrectly, as though they had been there untouched since 1947. Things have moved on since then and the Club has ensured that heritage and tradition are firmly entrenched within its walls, and have been zealously guarded and upheld by generations of members. The Club has grown from strength to strength over the years and can proudly claim to be one of the finest Clubs in the country with over 700 members and a membership base from all major cities in India.

The Ooty Hunt assembles on the steps of the Club.

The term 'snooker' was given to the game by Colonel Sir Neville Chamberlain[29] in 1875 whilst serving in the Army. In the Officers' Mess at Jubbulpore in India, gambling games such as pyramids, life pool and black pool were popular, with fifteen reds and a black used in the latter. To these were added yellow, green and pink, with blue and brown introduced some years later. One afternoon, Chamberlain's Devonshire regiment was visited by a young officer who had been trained at the Royal Military Academy in Woolwich. This officer explained that a first-year cadet at the Academy was

---

[29] Sir Neville Francis Fitzgerald Chamberlain KCB, KCVO, KPM.

referred to as a 'snooker'. Later, when one of the players failed to hole a coloured ball, Chamberlain shouted to him: 'Why, you're a regular snooker.' He then pointed out the meaning and that they were all 'snookers' at the game. The name was adopted for the game itself.

The Billiards Room at the Ooty Club where the Rules of Snooker were posted in 1882.

Chamberlain himself joined the Central India Horse in 1876, taking the game with him. After being wounded in the Afghan War, he moved to Ootacamund and the game became the speciality of the 'Ooty Club', and the first official set of rules for snooker were drafted in 1882 and were posted in the billiards room.

John Roberts (Junior), who was then Billiards Champion, visited India in 1885, met Chamberlain at dinner with the Maharajah of Cooch Behar and enquired about the rules of snooker. He then introduced the game into England, although it was many years before it became widely played there.

Bilateral exercise with Indian Navy and the Lakkshadweeps

In October 1995 HMS MONMOUTH, the sixth "Duke" -class Type 23 frigate of the Royal Navy arrived in Cochin to lead the British component of the largest Anglo-Indian naval exercise for thirty years. Affectionately known as 'The Black Duke', MONMOUTH is the only ship in service with the Royal Navy that has its name painted in black and flies a plain black flag in addition to the ensign. This is due to the dissolution of the title and the blacking out of the Coat of Arms of the Duke of Monmouth in 1685 following the Monmouth Rebellion against James II of England.

HMS MONMOUTH arrives in Cochin.

When I realised that the Indian Navy was drafting in a Rear Admiral to lead their team, I contacted the Admiralty to see if we could manage to mirror their effort, especially since the MONMOUTH was commanded by a Commander. The reply came winging back across the ether as an emphatic 'No', adding that there were no spare Rear-Admirals, but they were prepared to send out a Captain to lead the UK group. I had never met their nominee, Captain Billson but I contacted him at home in England, explained the situation and how keen I was that we should have a very senior officer as our Officer in Command. I asked him to provide himself with Commodore's epaulettes and a Commodore's ensign, to be flown from his 'flagship', the MONMOUTH. When he asked me how I was going to arrange for his sudden promotion, I explained that as the senior British RN officer in India, I was entitled to promote personnel on the 'Acting Unpaid' basis whenever I chose. This was of course absolute rubbish, but I felt justified, nevertheless.

The exercise went really well from the UK perspective and Commodore Billson appeared to enjoy his tour of duty in his new-found rank, albeit he was only a Commodore for one day. When the exercise completed, the plan was for the Commodore and I, to disembark from MONMOUTH by helicopter, to the island of Agatti in the Lakshadweep Islands, where the Indian Admiral would join us and all three of us would return to Cochin[30] by a coastguard fixed-wing aircraft.

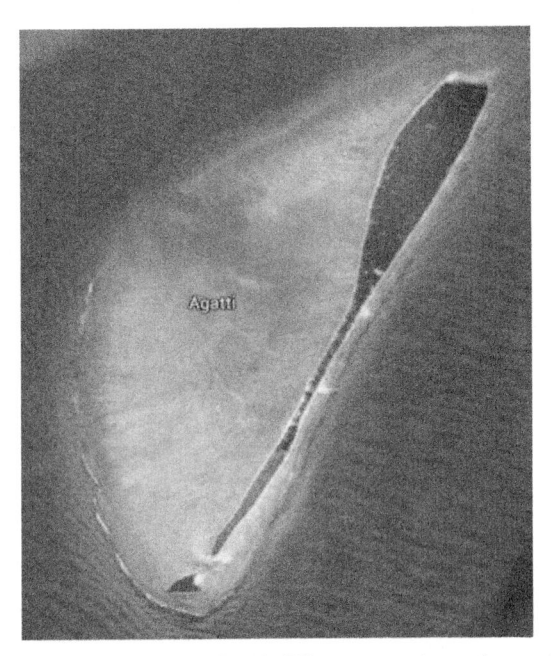

Agatti Island from Google Earth. The runway is at the southern tip.

---

[30] Now renamed Kochi.

MY BAGS ARE IN THE BACK

Agatti runway.

When we landed, both in uniform, we were met by a very smartly dressed Indian, wearing an ancient and shiny fireman's helmet, who, apart from his slender physique and Asian appearance, bore a remarkable resemblance to Benny Hill. He then asked us if we would like to inspect the fire engine parked a few yards away on the short walk to the airport building. Yet again, the Commodore carried out this duty with his customary charm and we then turned towards the airport buildings, hoping to find some respite from the amazing heat. This was not to be, however, since Benny Hill asked us if we could wait just a couple of minutes, while he went ahead to make sure everything was ready for us, his VIP visitors.

We waited, cooking slowly, and noticed that Benny had run round to the rear of the building. The two minutes passed and then the front door of the airport was opened and we were invited in. We were met by an Indian wearing a very smart airport official's peaked cap, with the title, 'Manager', nicely embroidered. After the customary 'Namaste', he reached towards the desk by his side and, with a flourish, produced a frightening looking Parang machete, accompanied by the most beautiful smile. I would like to say that neither of us flinched, but that would not quite be true. His next retrieval from the desk allayed our fears as he turned holding a massive coconut, which he then held at waist height, and split asunder, with one mighty swipe of the fearsome machete, with no apparent damage to his hand.

Having sampled the coconut, we exchanged pleasantries, while waiting for the arrival of the Indian Admiral and the coastguard aircraft and I then realised that not only did the manager look exactly like Benny Hill, but he sounded the same as well. I was tempted to ask the manager if we could see the fireman again to thank him for his services, but this was pre-empted by the arrival of the Indian helicopter. We all returned to Cochin, 286 miles to the west of the island and as we landed at the Naval airbase, we spotted the Indian helicopter, from one of their ships, which had diverted to Cochin during the night when unfortunately the pilot had lost contact with his mother-ship. The look on the Admiral's face said it all and he was very definitely not amused. The Commodore and I exchanged glances and felt sorry for the young pilot.

Commodore Geoffrey Billson's splendid sketch.

We became good friends and I discovered he had a well-developed skill as an artist and before he left he presented me with one of his cartoons, which made some clever references to a few lighter moments during the exercise. The morose helicopter pilot is self-explanatory, as is the fire brigade notice. The split coconut is evident, and there is a very obvious reference to some Naval Adviser taking pictures in front of the warning sign banning such activity.

My picture of the island, as we departed, is below.

The northern end of Agatti island as we depart.

There was one other moment during this exercise, which caused me some amusement as well as serving as a final recollection of my naval service. During the early evening of the exercise, I received an invitation from the Senior Ratings mess in MONMOUTH to join them after dinner at about 2000. As was the custom, even for a senior officer, I asked the Commanding Officer's permission and when he approved, joined the Chief and Fleet Chief Petty Officers in their mess. After a while, the Master at Arms took me to one side for a private chat.

"Is it true, Sir," he enquired, "that this is your last job in the Navy?"

I replied that indeed it was and he continued, "Is it also the case that Captains, on retirement, have a final lunch and a chat with the First Sea Lord?"

When I replied that that was indeed the case, he looked around and continued in a rather conspiratorial manner: "You see, Sir, the point is that we've had a vote here in the mess, Sir, and we've decided that someone's got to get a message to the First Sea Lord and I've drawn the short straw and been detailed off to ask if you could let him know our view on a very delicate matter, Sir."

This led to the obvious question as to what this 'delicate matter' could possibly be, that seemed to be causing such a clandestine approach, and this point I put to the Master at Arms.

At this, he paused and drew breath, and I imagined that he was going to tell me something frightfully personal, but he continued: "Well Sir, since you are definitely not going to be an Admiral, we want you to drop a word in for us. It's about these 'women at sea' you see Sir – It's not going to work you know, and someone's got to tell him and we have chosen you."

Postscript and the end of my Naval career

My wife, Lynn, and I did indeed have a farewell lunch with the First Sea Lord in his Admiralty Arch flat in early 1996 and afterwards I went to his office for a final meeting. Amongst other things, he asked me how many staff I had in India and when I demurred from telling him, he insisted, and I had, eventually, to tell him that it was a lot more than he had in London.

As to whether or not I raised the matter of 'women at sea', I will have to admit that my memory has become suddenly vague.

AUTHOR'S CAREER SUMMARY

CAPTAIN PETER GALLOWAY BSc, MSc, CEng, FIEE, FInstMgt, ROYAL NAVY

Born 16 December 1943

Joined the Royal Navy as a General List Engineer at BRNC Dartmouth on 17 September 1961.

After two years initial training at Dartmouth and at sea in the West Indies and the Far East, attended the RN Engineering College, Manadon in Plymouth for Graduate and Application training.

Qualified as Ship's Diver.

Service appointments included:

1969/1971	Guided Missile Destroyer, HMS HAMPSHIRE, High Power Engineer.
1972/1974	Admiralty Surface Weapons Establishment, Portsdown, Project Leader. Digital Gun System design.

Promoted Lieutenant Commander in 1974

1975/1977	Leander Class Frigate, HMS ACHILLES, Weapons Electrical Officer.
1978/1979	HMS CENTURION, Systems Analyst, Functional Costing System.

1979	Admiralty Underwater Weapons Establishment Portland, Deputy Project Manager, British Underwater Technical Evaluation Centre.

Promoted Commander in 1979

1980/1981	MOD, Directorate Naval Management Systems, Data Processing Policy.
1982/1983	HMS GLAMORGAN, Weapon Engineering Officer – served during the Falklands Conflict when the ship suffered extensive damage following an Exocet attack.
1984/1986	MOD, Naval Secretary, Weapon Engineering Commanders' Appointer
1986/1987	Admiralty Interview Board, Board Member & later as Board President.

Promoted to Captain in 1987

1988	New Delhi, Student at the National Defence College.
1989	MOD, Ordnance Board, as Board Member.
1990/1992	MOD, Directorate of Science (Sea), Deputy Director.
1993/1995	New Delhi, Naval Adviser to the British High Commissioner.

Retired from Royal Navy in 1996. Spent further 8 years marketing RN training in Middle East.

Now living in the South of England with his wife Lynn. They were married in 1965, have two grown up happily married children and four simply wonderful grandchildren.

Printed in Great Britain
by Amazon